One of the major pillars of our research at the National Center for Fathering is modeling. Tony and Lois are not only great communicators on the message of marriage, they truly model kingdom marriage. I love how Tony defines kingdom marriage as, "connecting God's purpose with your pleasure." This book is a most excellent blueprint for building a strong marriage—and God loves marriage.

CAREY AND MELANIE CASEY
National Center for Fathering

What exactly does it mean to have a "kingdom perspective" on marriage? Dr. Tony Evans answers that question with pastoral insight and biblical wisdom in this engaging new book. *Kingdom Marriage* is essential reading for husbands and wives who want to make their relationship the best it can be for the sake of the Kingdom.

DR. GREG SMALLEY
Vice president of Marriage and Family Formation, Focus on the Family

In the midst of a cultural battle on marriage, Dr. Tony Evans has clearly identified the importance of reorienting our hearts toward God's kingdom. This fresh biblical perspective is like a much needed "realignment" for our relationships.

TIM POPADIC
President, Relationship Enrichment Collaborative and executive producer of the Date Night Comedy Tour

Kingdom Marriage is a book that'll influence my own marriage for a very long time! When it comes to our marriage, there's so much more going on than meets the eye. Pastor Evans unveils scripturally so much of what we cannot see, and he does it in a way that somehow leaves you convicted but motivated to act, all at the same time. Get the angels summoned on your behalf. Find the true purpose of what your marriage was meant to be. Be more fulfilled in your marriage than you ever dreamed possible. That's a legacy worth leaving to your kids.

JOSHUA STRAUB, PH.D.
Author, *Safe House: How Emotional Safety Is the Key to Raising Kids Who Live, Love, and Lead Well*

Tony Evans is without a doubt truly one of the greatest communicators of the twentieth and twenty-first centuries! The reason he speaks and writes so well is because his heart is 100 percent committed to serving Jesus and making Him known to the world. I highly recommend this book because any part of Tony Evans that you or I can receive will make us a much better person, a better spouse, and a greater person of knowing a relationship with Jesus Christ.

JOE WHITE
President, Kanakuk Ministries

I daresay *Kingdom Marriage* will be unlike any marriage book you've read all year. Ninety percent of marriage books focus on the human element; *Kingdom Marriage* takes you where very few marriage books go: straight into the spiritual realm. Dr. Tony Evans talks about spiritual warfare, spiritual purpose, spiritual strongholds, and much, much more. If you've read fifty marriage books, you still need to read this one, as it is unlike all the others. The chapter on restoration alone is worth the price of the entire book. Masterfully done, prophetically alive, and biblically true, *Kingdom Marriage* is a tour de force for couples who want to become more spiritually aware in their marriage.

GARY THOMAS
Author, *Sacred Marriage* and *A Lifelong Love*

We love this book! *Kingdom Marriage* is perfect for couples like us who need to be reminded of the biblical, historical, and current truth about how marriage was designed by God. Every couple should read this book and give it as a gift to others they care about.

SCOTT AND BETHANY PALMER
The Money Couple

Whether you are engaged to be married or you've been married for sixty years, you should read this book with your spouse. *Kingdom Marriage* will give you the wisdom and practical insight to make your marriage what God intended it to be—not just a social contract, but a sacred covenant.

RACHEL CRUZE
New York Times best-selling author and personal finance expert

KINGDOM
MARRIAGE

TONY EVANS
KINGDOM
MARRIAGE

CONNECTING GOD'S PURPOSE
WITH YOUR PLEASURE

TYNDALE HOUSE PUBLISHERS, INC.
CAROL STREAM, ILLINOIS

Kingdom Marriage: Connecting God's Purpose with Your Pleasure
© 2016 Tony Evans

A Focus on the Family book published by Tyndale House Publishers, Inc., Carol Stream, Illinois 60188

Focus on the Family and the accompanying logo and design are federally registered trademarks of Focus on the Family, 8605 Explorer Drive, Colorado Springs, CO 80920.

TYNDALE and Tyndale's quill logo are registered trademarks of Tyndale House Publishers, Inc.

Cover design by Jennifer Ghionzoli

Photograph of couple copyright © Stephen Vosloo. All rights reserved.
Photograph of hair copyright © BonninStudio/Stocksy. All rights reserved.
Background photograph of landscape copyright © Morgan Sessions/Unsplash.com. All rights reserved.

Library of Congress Cataloging-in-Publication Data

Names: Evans, Tony, 1949- author.
Title: Kingdom marriage : connecting God's purpose with your pleasure / Dr. Tony Evans.
Description: First Edition. | Carol Stream, Illinois : Tyndale House Publishers, 2016. | "A Focus on the Family book." | Includes bibliographical references and index.
Identifiers: LCCN 2016016615 | ISBN 9781589978201 (alk. paper)
Subjects: LCSH: Marriage—Religious aspects—Christianity.
Classification: LCC BT706 .E93 2016 | DDC 248.8/44—dc23
LC record available at https://lccn.loc.gov/2016016615

Printed in the United States of America

22   21   20   19   18   17   16

7   6   5   4   3   2

This book is gratefully and lovingly dedicated to my wife, Lois, for all the love, support, skill, sacrifice, and encouragement she has given me. This has served as the foundation for all that God has allowed me to accomplish. You are most certainly the wind beneath my wings.

CONTENTS

PART I:
THE FOUNDATION OF A KINGDOM MARRIAGE

PART II:
THE FUNCTION OF A KINGDOM MARRIAGE

PART I

✦✦✦✦✦✦✦

The Foundation of a
KINGDOM
MARRIAGE

1

❖❖❖❖❖❖

ORIGIN

A KINGDOM MARRIAGE not only shares passion, but more important, it has a purpose.

Passion matters and happiness is great, but rather than being the purposes for marriage, they are benefits. Marriage exists to glorify God by expanding His rule and reach. It uniquely reflects His image like nothing else. When you pursue God's purpose as a couple, then everything else you value in life—such as happiness, love, and satisfaction—will fall into place.

> ❖❖❖❖
> *The absence of a kingdom purpose for marriage makes it appear as if many couples have been married by the secretary of war rather than the justice of the peace.*
> ❖❖❖❖

The absence of a kingdom purpose for marriage makes it appear as if many couples have been married by the secretary of war rather than the justice of the peace. A passenger on a plane one day noticed that the man sitting next to him had his wedding ring on the wrong hand, so he asked him why. The husband replied, "Because I married the wrong woman."

Far too many couples today feel that marriage has turned into too much trouble, like the man who said, "My wife and I were happy for twenty years. And then we got married."

Friend, when God established marriage, He established it to last. It is only when we have removed ourselves from His purpose for our relationships that we face the untimely unraveling of what was meant to be permanently satisfying.

A young girl was entertaining herself by playing with her grandmother's hands. When she asked why her grandmother's wedding ring was so large and gaudy, the grandmother sighed and then smiled and said, "Child, it's because when I got married, rings were made to last."

The problem today is that we have transposed the benefit of marriage with the goal, so that when the benefit—happiness—is not working out, we quit and move on, or we resign ourselves to living a life of unhappiness. A large percentage of marriages end in divorce, and many couples who remain together do so out of economic or practical constraints, not love and a shared purpose. Again, kingdom couples share a purpose, not just passion. Emotions change, but the purpose remains and is what can tie two people together until death do they part.

Most people subscribe to the popular notion of marriage that begins when two people fall in love and share an emotional experience identified by chills, thrills, and butterflies. With eyes only for each other, the infatuated pair promise undying love at the altar only to discover that after they say "I do," they just don't anymore. Divorce seems like the only way to forge a truce. In fact, many men and women tell their biggest lies on their wedding days. They promise to "love, honor, and cherish" in sickness and in health, for richer or poorer, for better or worse, for as long as they both shall live. Then, before long, they are divorced or wish they were. If religion is part and parcel of the relationship, many couples will stay together for the sake of the kids. Yet they do so in loveless environments punctuated by conflict, selfishness, and the opposite of the true image of God.

> *Marriage is not merely a social contract; it is a sacred covenant. It is not simply a means of looking for love, happiness, and fulfillment.*

When children grow up in loveless homes, they don't learn the crucial lessons necessary to develop good self-images now and to build strong marriages for themselves later. When kids witness their dads coercing or demanding submission from their moms, they take on a warped definition of manhood and womanhood, which often results in poor behavior and communication later in life.

Our marriages today are crumbling at such a high rate not because we no longer get along but because we have lost sight of the blessing tied to biblical marriage. Marriage is not merely a social contract; it is a sacred covenant. It is not simply a means of looking for love, happiness, and fulfillment. Those things are important; in fact, they are critical. But they are not the most important or the most critical. Yet because we have put second things first, as important as second things are, we are having trouble living out either. When God's purpose and principles for marriage are undermined, His image becomes distorted, and our ability to influence others on God's behalf erodes.

Kingdom couples must view marriage through God's kingdom lens. A *kingdom marriage* is defined as "a covenantal union between a man and a woman who commit themselves to function in unison under divine authority in order to replicate God's image and expand His rule in the world through both their individual and joint callings."

A Lasting Tribute

Victoria's father died when she was only one. Raised in a single-parent household, Victoria didn't have a model of marriage to follow. Her relationship with her mom was strained at the best of times, and they were completely estranged as she grew older. Tossed here and there to different places and people, Victoria grew up in a contradictory world that provided little direction and consistency. What hope would she have of finding a happy home?

At the age of eighteen, Victoria faced new responsibilities. She was crowned Queen of England, something few people expected, since she wasn't first in line for the throne. However, the two men before her had died, and she found herself receiving a title at a time when it meant precious little. The English monarchy was in question, carried no real influence, and sat precariously on a line between honor and contempt. It was the early 1800s, and one of the wealthiest and most powerful nations in the world had a teenager as its queen.

Yet just a few years later, Victoria married the man who would help her change the face of the monarchy for good. His name was Albert, and funny enough, *she* proposed to *him*. (Since she was the queen, he was not allowed to propose to her.) They soon married, and her diary and accounts reveal that they were deeply in love from the start. Later she wrote, "Without him everything loses its interest."[1]

Their marriage stayed strong and lasted until Albert's untimely death in his early forties. Yet even though it was short, what their marriage produced was nothing short of remarkable. It not only strengthened Victoria's rule, as Albert became his wife's chief adviser and promoter, but it also expanded the dominion and rule of their nation throughout the rest of the continent through their children. Victoria and Albert raised their children with a kingdom mind-set.

German by birth, Prince Albert was considered an invading foreigner and "British interloper" by most. Yet he became a respected leader in the nation as he honored Victoria's position and strength while seeking the good of her career and nation through his influence in political and domestic issues.[2] The view of the monarchy completely changed by the end of Queen Victoria's reign, and it came to be known as a powerful tool for good for the land. The nine children the couple raised likewise went on to increase the reach of that good into countries near and far.

Each of their nine children, and many of their forty-two grandchildren, married into royal families. This included a German empress and queen of Prussia, a king of England, a grand duchess who was a champion of women's causes and a promoter of female nursing, a cofounder of the Red Cross who also married into German royalty, the wife of a governor general of Canada, a Canadian commander in chief, and various other influential leaders.[3]

While it is widely purported that Victoria valued her marriage far more than she valued her parenting role,[4] she and Albert took their duties to pass on their dominion and legacy seriously, and they were effective. In that, and much more, their marital success contributed to the success not only of England's citizens but also of people throughout the world who were positively impacted by the improvements in women's rights, social services, and the attention to peace their leaders sought.

But what happened after their marriage ended impresses me most about the love and strength of their union. Following Albert's untimely death, the queen showed him the greatest honor any wife could give. Victoria was still young when widowed, and she could have had any royal suitor in the world. Yet she chose to remain in mourning over the loss of the love of her life. For four decades, Queen Victoria clothed herself daily in black, staying true to the memory of her marriage even after death had parted them. Many thought her grief was excessive, but Victoria's love for Albert demanded nothing less. I have found no greater testament to a spouse's love than what the queen unwaveringly gave to her prince.

> *We should seek to honor each other no less, to love each other no less, and to expand God's dominion and rule no less through all we do in our marriages.*

Queen Victoria and Prince Albert shared the fruit of happiness in marriage despite the obvious challenges of a large family, the pressures of duty and office, and certain male-female sensitivities resulting from her superior role. Yet they did it all successfully while carrying out the mission of expanding their dominion and influence upon the world.

As followers of the one true King over all, we should seek to honor each other no less, to love each other no less, and to expand God's dominion and rule no less through all we do in our marriages.

The King and His Kingdom

The key to influencing our society and world with lasting impact is found in solidifying biblical marriage in the way God intended. It starts with both wife and husband reflecting God and His image and modeling that reflection within the roles and responsibilities of their union. This begins with a correct understanding of God's kingdom and their responsibilities in it.

Yet because the body of Christ in America has focused much more heavily on buildings, programs, and entertainment, far too few have a full understanding of God's kingdom or what biblical commitment looks like.

To gain some background, let me begin by stating that if you are an American, you are most likely an American because you were born here. If you are a part of the kingdom of God, it is because you have been born again into His kingdom through personal faith in the death, burial, and resurrection of the sinless Savior, Jesus Christ.

Understanding the kingdom with regard to your marriage is the key to understanding the Bible.

Understanding the Kingdom with regard to your marriage is the key to understanding the Bible. The unifying, central theme throughout the Bible—from Genesis to Revelation—is the glory of God and the advancement of His kingdom.

When we lack an integration of the kingdom theme in our Bible study and application, the Bible becomes a collection of disconnected stories that are great for information and inspiration but seem unrelated in purpose, direction, and contemporary relevance. Scripture exists to highlight God's movement in history. It shows us the connection of the Kingdom. Fully grasping this concept makes this several-thousand-year-old manuscript relevant to our day-to-day decisions. The Kingdom is not only then; it is also now.

The closer God and His rule are tied to the definition of marriage, the more order, productivity, and fulfillment are experienced in our marriages. The further away God and His rule are, the more chaos occurs in the home.

What is the kingdom? Throughout the Bible, the kingdom of God is His rule. The Greek word used for "kingdom" is *basileia*, translated "rule" or "authority." Any kingdom consists of three crucial components: First, there is a ruler; second, a realm of subjects who fall underneath this rule; and third, the rules of governance. God's kingdom is the authoritative execution of His comprehensive governance over all creation. His kingdom is all-encompassing. It covers everything that exists.

The universe we live in is a theocracy. *Theos* refers to God, and *ocracy* refers to rule. A kingdom perspective means that the rule of God (theocracy) trumps the rule of man (homocracy). Scripture expresses it this way: "The LORD has established his throne in heaven, and his kingdom rules over all" (Psalm 103:19, NIV).

God's kingdom is larger than the temporal, governmental, and social realms that make up our world. It is not confined to the walls of the church in which we call on His name in a corporate setting. The kingdom is both now (Mark 1:15) and not yet (Matthew 16:28). It is not only near (Luke 17:21) but also far (Matthew 7:21). Jesus spoke to the heavenly origin of His earthly kingdom shortly before His crucifixion, when He responded to Pilate,

> My kingdom is not of this world. If My kingdom were of this world, then My servants would be fighting so that I would not be handed over to the Jews; but as it is, My kingdom is not of this realm. (John 18:36)

God's kingdom consists of covenantal institutions that include the family, the church, and civil government (the state). God rules them all, and each is accountable to Him and His standards as their sovereign, regardless of whether they recognize that rule. Failure to function under His authority produces chaos and consequences similar to what Adam and Eve experienced in the garden and what we see all around us today.

The foundation of civilization is the family, and the foundation of the family is marriage. Therefore the destruction of marriage naturally results in the destruction of civilization, which is why it is critical that we make strengthening marriages and families an integral part of the church's mission.

All three covenantal institutions (family, church, and civil government) were designed to operate on a standard of absolute truth.

All three covenantal institutions (family, church, and civil government) were designed to operate on a standard of absolute truth. We see this show up first in the garden when God told Adam and Eve that they could eat freely from any tree *except* the Tree of the Knowledge of Good and Evil. God wanted His revelation and not human opinion to be the basis and foundation for their relationship. When they ate of this tree, they removed themselves from the absolute nature of God's command, ushering reason into their future equations. As a result, today we must be careful to always place our reasoning underneath the umbrella of absolute, revealed truth. Truth is fundamentally God-based knowledge. This standard of truth is nonnegotiable, transcending cultural, economic, belief-based, and situational lines.

Not only does the Kingdom agenda operate on this foundation of absolute truth, but it also operates under the only all-inclusive principle presented to us for understanding the work of God and His kingdom. This principle is His glory. Romans 11:36 says that "from Him and through Him and to Him are all things. To Him be the glory forever. Amen."

Glory denotes significance and value. Since everything originates from God, takes place through God, and goes to God, God's glory exists intrinsically in Himself. Whether we ascribe glory to God or not is irrelevant to the amount of glory God has. His glory is already fully present in Him. Yet the degree to which we personally experience and access God's glory in our lives, our marriages, and our homes is found in the extent to which we align ourselves under His comprehensive rule. When we align our lives under God and His rule, He radiates and magnifies His glory to, in, and through us. We experience the abundant life and abundant marriages Christ came to secure on our behalf (John 10:10).

> *For the Kingdom agenda to be made manifest in your marriage, it calls for aligning all you do, think, and say under God's rule.*

The number one way to bring God glory is by surrendering to His sovereign rule. This acknowledges His supremacy over every area of our lives. When we operate in our marriages based on these principles of the Kingdom agenda, we are free to experience God's hand of blessing and His promise to work all things together for good (Romans 8:28).

Conversely, when we do not operate according to God's kingdom and His rule over our lives, we limit our opportunity to experience His hand working all things together for good. This is because we have chosen to define God according to our purpose rather than His. But God will be defined by no one but Himself. It is the rule of God (theocracy) and not the rule of man (homocracy) that is paramount. If God's kingdom is comprehensive, as we have seen, so is His Kingdom agenda. The *Kingdom agenda* may be defined as "the visible manifestation of the comprehensive rule of God over every area of life." For the Kingdom agenda to be made manifest in your marriage, it calls for aligning all you do, think, and say under God's rule. When that is done, you will experience the fruit of all the good that God has planned for you.

The reason so many of us are struggling as believers is that instead of fulfilling *His* agenda, we want God to bless *our* agendas for our marriages. We want God to okay our plans rather than our fulfilling His. We want God to bring us glory rather than our bringing Him glory through honoring the marriage covenant as He intended it.

The Purpose of Marriage

God established marriage in a perfect environment. In fact, marriage came before sin. God created the first family and gave them His blessing, His commission, and His image:

> Then God said, "Let Us make man in Our image, according to Our likeness; and let them rule over the fish of the sea and over the birds of the sky and over the cattle and over all the earth, and over every creeping thing that creeps on the earth." God created man in His own image, in the image of God He created him; male and female He created them. God blessed them; and God said to them, "Be fruitful and multiply, and fill the earth, and subdue it; and rule over the fish of the sea and over the birds of the sky and over every living thing that moves on the earth." (Genesis 1:26–28)

As we see from the outset of this foundational passage on marriage, Adam and Eve were to reflect the triune image of God—unity in the midst of diversity. An image mirrors that which it reflects; it doesn't add to, take away from, or distort. God created humanity as His mirror and called for that mirror to reproduce more mirrors through marriage. The marriage union—made up of male and female—most fully expresses who God truly is, and it is the most comprehensive manifestation of His image.

Our goal as married couples is not only to mirror God in the visible realm predicated on His reality in the invisible realm, but also to transfer the perfection of that image to our children as we raise kingdom kids. Simply put, the mission of marriage is to manifest and replicate the image of God in history, as well as to carry out His divinely mandated dominion ("let them rule"). Dominion essentially means ruling on God's behalf in history so that history comes underneath God's authority. The blessings God promised, and that we so desire to experience in marriage, were to be the outgrowth of men and women fulfilling God's purpose of reflecting His image and managing together His creation under His rule. Happiness is to be a benefit of a strong marriage but not the goal. The goal of marriage is to reflect God through the advancement of His kingdom on earth. Happiness occurs as an organic outgrowth when this goal is pursued.

The Dominion of Husband and Wife

In Genesis 1:28, God gave Adam and Eve the commission to rule. Understanding this passage is critical to the success of a kingdom marriage. To do so, let's look at the historical context within which the family was first placed.

God's creation of humanity came after the rebellion of Satan as a way of setting the human race to rule over God's created order. We see this in Psalm 8:3–6:

When I consider Your heavens, the work of Your fingers,
The moon and the stars, which You have ordained;
What is man that You take thought of him,
And the son of man that You care for him?
Yet You have made him a little lower than God,
And You crown him with glory and majesty!
You make him to rule over the works of Your hands;
You have put all things under his feet.

The commission to "let them rule over the fish of the sea and over the birds of the sky and over the cattle and over all the earth" (Genesis 1:26) was partnered with the command to "subdue" the earth (verse 28). In formal theology we refer to this as the *Dominion Covenant*.

The backstory to this covenant was the rebellion of Satan against the kingdom of God, which resulted in the banishment of Satan and his fallen angels to earth prior to their permanent incarceration in hell. Humankind, and the institution of marriage, was specially created for people to have a relationship with God and each other that would result in a demonstration of God's greater glory and the superiority of His kingdom through humanity. This goal and the blessings connected to it could only be achieved, however, if the marriage relationship operated according to its divine design, which explains why Satan didn't attack Adam until he was married.

> *Dominion essentially means ruling on God's behalf in history so that history comes underneath God's authority.*

God established a kingdom on earth that would rule over and defeat the kingdom of Satan. When Christ comes to create His millennial kingdom, it will be the final, triumphant declaration of God's glory. Satan will then be locked up during that time to reveal his ultimate defeat and judgment (Revelation 20:1–3).

Yet, for now, God has issued a purpose for you and me—and for married couples especially—to harness and rule a part of His creation. Every person was created with that divine intent, and every marital union exists to pass down that intent to the next generation. In summary, the marriage relationship is to rule and replicate the image and kingdom of God in history.

When God established the first family and gave them dominion to rule, He stated that He would not rule independently of them. Our decisions on earth would impact His decisions from heaven (Ephesians 3:10). God did this for one reason: to demonstrate to Satan and his minions that He can do more to manifest His glory through lesser creatures than through the once shining star.

We often think that a battle is taking place between God and Satan these days. But there is no battle going on between them. No battle can exist between the Creator and a created one. That would be similar to me saying I'll take on

Manny Pacquiao in the ring. Sure, we both might step forward to fight, but I'd be out like a light at the first punch.

Satan, a created creature, is no match for the all-powerful Creator. That's no fight. Yet what God did establish was the opportunity for inferior creatures—human beings (Psalm 8:5)—to demonstrate that in this spiritual battle, even we can win when we operate according to God's kingdom rule. We are in an ongoing battle, and Satan has had thousands of years to perfect his punches. He likes to target married couples first, since we ultimately reflect the union of Christ with the church, as well as pass down the image of God to the next generation. As kingdom couples, we have been cast in a cosmic conflict to manifest God's rule in history for the advancement of His kingdom and the reflection of His glory.

God has delegated the managerial responsibility for ruling on earth. We hold that responsibility. Yet keep in mind that He has not turned over *absolute* ownership of the earth to us. By turning over the management to us, He has established a process, within certain boundaries, wherein He respects our decisions even if they go against His own, or even if those decisions are not in the best interest of that which is being managed. As a result, we either experience blessing or the consequences of poor decisions.

> ❖❖❖❖❖
>
> *God has delegated the managerial responsibility for ruling on earth. We hold that responsibility.*
>
> ❖❖❖❖❖

God is the ultimate owner over all. But He has delegated management duties, under His sovereignty, to us. Your decisions as a couple regarding both how you relate to each other and how you reflect God to others through your union directly affect the quality of life you experience. The tragedy for most couples is that they have followed suit with Satan, seeking ownership rights, not just management responsibilities. As owners, couples go outside of God's rule and make decisions based on their preferred will or desires. And like Satan, they experience the distance and conflict he did when he was booted from God's presence.

What that means is that you can have a happy marriage or a miserable marriage depending on whether or not you exercise your rule as a reflection of God's image. God isn't going to make you rule according to His rule. He isn't going to force you to have a productive and fulfilling relationship. He established marriage and its purposes, but you have the option of living by those purposes or not.

Frequently the well-being of a marriage is determined by whether a man and a woman are reflecting God's image in their individual roles. Once that mirror shatters or even cracks, the reflection of the relationship breaks with it. Nearly every time there's a family breakdown, it is the result of one or both spouses operating outside the covenantal bonds of marriage. They are modeling a broken mirror. As a result, they experience less of God's favor.

❖❖❖❖❖

When we as couples fail to align ourselves under God's kingdom rule, the battle lines are drawn.

❖❖❖❖❖

Satan either tries to get us to relinquish our management and hand it over to him by deceiving us into believing that he has authority, or he tries to get us to manage poorly based on our own judgments and distorted worldviews. He often does this through the promotion of conflict in our relationships, or through the enticement of ungodly choices.

When we as couples fail to align ourselves under God's kingdom rule, the battle lines are drawn.

Self-centered viewpoints like those create tension in a marriage. But the problems and challenges that marriages face should cause us to seek and apply the power of God, not divorce our spouses.

I've been the chaplain for the NBA's Dallas Mavericks for more than three decades. I enjoy a good game of basketball as much as the next person. And I'm pretty good at playing basketball—pretty much unstoppable . . . when I play alone. When unopposed, I can make any play and grab nothing but net. Yet in my younger days when I had an opportunity to play against the former Mavs star forward, Mark Aguirre, I quickly discovered I wasn't that great at basketball after all. The true test of my ball skills came only when I faced opposition.

So it is with marriage. But conflict, struggle, challenge, and differences shouldn't destroy our union; they should show the power of Christ within us. Jesus never asks you as a married couple to do what He has not already given you the ability to do (Philippians 4:13). Marriage is one of the greatest ways you can show the difference that Jesus Christ makes. You can reflect the glory of God and the unity of the Trinity through your shared purpose, honor, and love as a true kingdom couple. When you do that, you will not only have a love story for the ages, like Queen Victoria and Prince Albert, but you will also expand God's dominion and rule on earth through your marriage and your legacy. The bottom line is that marriage is a kingdom concept, not merely a social one.

When my wife, Lois, and I met, fell in love, and began to discuss marriage, a large part of our planning revolved around how God could use our relationship to bring Him glory and serve His kingdom. Since we were both committed to Christ and were called to serve Him, it was natural to include God's kingdom purpose as the defining centerpiece of our relationship. This is the orientation God wants every couple to enter marriage with. The key question is this: How can our marriages reflect God's image and advance His kingdom? As that question is answered, our marriages can expect the blessings and joy that we so deeply long for.

It was clear in the establishment of marriage that God wanted the institution sovereignly under His control and existing for His purpose. Thus, it was God who created man. It was God who communicated to man His Word. It was God who revealed the need in man for a woman. It was God who created the woman from the man. It was God who brought the woman to the man. So it was clearly God's intent that He never be left out of marriage, but rather be the definition of it.

2

❖❖❖❖❖

ORDER

I'VE NEVER LIVED OVERSEAS, but I know Americans who have, and I've had the opportunity to travel abroad extensively over the past several decades. One thing always startles me more than anything else in some of the underdeveloped countries I have visited: the way people drive.

In some places it feels as though everyone has been cast in the latest *Fast and Furious* film. In other places, I'm not sure who owns the roads—bicycles, vehicles, or animals. More often than not, it is difficult for me to even determine where the lanes are. Sometimes they aren't marked, and cars, public-transportation vehicles, and bikes swerve in and out of each other's way. Toss a few pedestrians in there, and it's a recipe for chaos.

Having experienced this firsthand, I'm not surprised that, according to government reports, car accidents rather than terrorism, crime, or even natural disasters claimed more American lives abroad from 2011 through 2013 than anything else.[1] Between twenty and fifty million people suffer from nonfatal injuries as a result of car accidents each year. And road accidents are considered to be the eighth leading cause of death globally, right up there with diseases like malaria.[2] A lack of clear lane delineation, as well as a lack of adherence to the lanes, causes many of these accidents.

Take a moment to imagine yourself driving in rush-hour traffic in the largest city near you. It's stressful enough just driving in that, isn't it? Toss in some construction barrels, as well as a few potholes, and now it's even more stressful. But remove the lanes markers altogether? Now, would driving even be possible? I doubt it. There would probably be a pileup within a matter of minutes, and a traffic jam for miles on end.

Without order there is chaos, which is why Satan continually tries to stir things up in our marriages. As long as chaos reigns, we can never move into a place of order, peace, harmony, and progress. God has ordained a rulership for you and your spouse to carry out. He has intentionally brought the two of you together to fulfill His purpose for your lives. Yet just as you wouldn't be able to drive in rush-hour traffic without following clearly marked lanes, neither can you move forward to carry out all God has in store for you as a couple without following the lanes of His prescribed order. Satan knows that if he is going to cancel out your capacity to rule, he has to disrupt order by creating dissension and division.

Whatever Satan can divide, he can control. That's especially true in our marriages. This is exactly the approach he took when dividing Adam and Eve from each other and removing them from God's blessings. He got Eve to move outside her lane by questioning God's Word, and then he got Adam to move outside his lane by taking part in eating the fruit. When they removed themselves from their pre-scribed positions of alignment under God, they lost their ability to rule their world. Instead of enjoying the blessings God had promised, they now lived under a curse. The very things that had been designed to bring them good now brought them pain.

Without order there is chaos, which is why Satan continually tries to stir things up in our marriages.

Many couples today are living under the effects of a curse. They are no longer enjoying the blessings of God's favor but instead are suffering the conse-quences of their disobedience. Over the years God's Word has been so watered down and twisted to fit our cultural norms that many couples don't even real-ize why things are in the mess they're in. But if you will commit to applying God's prescribed order to your marriage relationship, you will begin to see the fruit of blessing showing up not only in your partnership but in other areas connected to your family as well. This happens as you open up the opportunity for greater favor to flow.

Headship Applies to Both Husband and Wife

We read about God's prescribed order in Paul's letter to the church at Corinth. If you know the history of the Corinthian church, you know that it was a church in chaos and disorder. Paul spoke into this chaos with a principle to set things straight: "I want you to understand that Christ is the head of every man, and the man is the head of a woman, and God is the head of Christ" (1 Corinthians 11:3). In this one verse we find the spiritual key to covering and authority that, when followed, can save any marriage. It can turn any deflated and defeated marriage into a victorious, productive one. Or it can give an already functioning relationship the power to pull off even greater exploits for the Lord.

When I counsel couples who are struggling in their marriages, without fail one or both of the spouses are no longer applying this principle in their lives. Get this one thing right, and all else will align underneath it.

Let's quickly walk through this principle, and then we'll talk about the rationale behind it as well as the ramifications. Whenever I teach on this subject, I always like to start from the end because it is the quickest point of tangible identification: God is the head of Christ.

Now we know theologically that Jesus is equal to God, so this reference to God as the head of Christ is inferring *position* rather than inequality. After all, Jesus is the eternal Son of God, and He possesses the full divine essence of all that makes God God. Christ's ontological being is the same as God in makeup; however, when it comes to functioning, Jesus comes underneath God in the order of carrying out the divine design and plan.

That's why when Jesus was on earth, He prayed, "Not My will, but Yours be done" (Luke 22:42). The work of redemption was accomplished because Jesus came underneath the headship of the Father, thus securing forgiveness, salvation, glorification, and eternal life for all who believe on Him.

Had Jesus rebelled as He prayed in the garden of Gethsemane because He felt that His rights were being infringed upon or His goals were being impeded, we would all be in a world of hurt right now. Rather, He submitted, and as a result we now have access to God through Him, as well as the abundant life He died to secure on our behalf.

Just as Christ is under God, we discover in 1 Corinthians 11:3 that every man is under Christ. Because Paul was writing to the church, he was referencing believers. Every Christian man has Jesus Christ in headship over him. This is a biblical truth as well as a foundational part of a healthy marriage that is rarely taught or addressed. So much teaching on the concept of submission focuses on the wife's submission to her husband, and yet in the very same verse is found the mandate for the husband's submission under Jesus Christ. No Christian man is autonomous. Every man is answerable to Christ. In fact, a *man* is defined biblically as "a male who has learned to submit his maleness to the lordship of Jesus Christ."

In the very same verse is found the mandate for the husband's submission under Jesus Christ.

If a husband expects his wife to answer to him, she should also see that modeled in her husband as he answers to Christ. Far too many men get out of their lanes with respect to Christ but expect their wives to be in their lanes with respect to them. No one should be shocked if a marriage ends in disarray when a man is not operating according to the principles of God. He's out of his lane. And if he's out of his lane, more than likely his wife is also out of her lane. A crash is going to occur when two people are not living in alignment with the divine order God has established.

Headship is often an area of confusion and questions for the couples I counsel. For the wife, there is a tangible human being to whom she is to submit. Yet for the husband, while Christ is real, He doesn't speak audibly, and much is left to the man's interpretation. This is unfortunate, and I believe that we have missed our calling as a church body to provide the accountability men need to both teach and guide as spiritual leaders in the church.

One couple I was recently counseling complained of arguing about nearly everything. While they sat in my office, I could see the distrust and defenses they had both put up. One said something, and the other corrected it. They seemed to be at an impasse on a lot of levels. I've known this couple for some time, and I truly wanted to see their marriage restored. I'm not able to do this for everyone I counsel, but I gave them my personal cell number and asked if they would agree to one thing: The next time they argued and couldn't reach a conclusion to their conflict, they would call me and allow me to hold them accountable in the situation based on God's Word.

Immediately after I said that, the wife broke down in tears. It was as if relief flooded over her. I'm not sure why, but based on my experience with many other couples I've counseled, I assume that she felt her husband's accountability to Christ meant nothing because no one was holding him to it. But now there would be an equal hearing between them both. The couple agreed, and I was grateful for the opportunity to intervene in a positive way.

The church was established as God's governing body on earth to strengthen its members so that we might advance His Kingdom agenda.

The church exists to provide that sounding board in conflict situations. At the church where I pastor, we have a ministry of marriage mentors. These are couples who have demonstrated a healthy relationship and level of commitment to each other and to the Lord over the years and who now volunteer to provide that accountability for Christ's headship in marriages that are faltering. The church is to be about so much more than simply preaching and singing on Sunday. The church was established as God's governing body on earth to strengthen its members so that we might advance His Kingdom agenda. Unfortunately, we've turned the church into a club or coffeehouse, and much of the significance of why it exists has been lost.

Husbands, you are accountable to God under Christ. I've seen marriages destroyed because the husband turned a blind eye to his own responsibility as protector, provider, nurturer, and preserver of the home while blaming his wife for any and all things. Had the husband stepped up and stayed in his lane, I have no doubt that God would have restored the marriage. Men, there is no excuse for holding your wife to a standard that you won't hold yourself to as well.

Have you ever driven a car that was out of alignment? A whole lot of shaking goes on when things are not lined up right. In addition, there's a whole lot of unnecessary wear and tear on the tires. The fundamental problem we face today in marriages is that men are out of alignment and then get upset because the ones following them (their wives and children) are out of line as well. You must be in alignment spiritually if you want those who are following you to be in line. To put it another way: Husbands, if you want your wives to call you "lord," then they need to see you calling Jesus Christ "Lord" and modeling Him.

Last, we read in 1 Corinthians that "the man is the head of a woman" (11:3). Since I'll be covering this in another chapter, I'll only touch on it briefly here. First, I want to point out that it says "a" woman. This is not a blanket declaration of male-over-female rule. This refers to the order of a marriage, and nothing more. The husband is over his wife in final authority, not in equality, ability, or even contribution. As a result of the man's headship, the wife comes under his provision, protection, and guidance. Headship carries with it a responsibility. The wife is to look to the husband (her head) for these things. She is to follow the husband's lead as her husband follows Christ's lead. This is the divine order.

Without spiritual authority, it is difficult to accomplish anything worthwhile, let alone experience a thriving marriage.

This is exactly what Satan shifted in the garden to bring about the curse. He went straight to Eve first because Adam had abdicated his role. This made it easy for Eve to abdicate hers as well when she took over the lead and gave instruction to Adam to eat the fruit. All hell broke loose in the garden because Adam and Eve got out of order.

As we see from their example, when headship is broken, authority is lost. Without spiritual authority, it is difficult to accomplish anything worthwhile, let alone experience a thriving marriage. The problems we are facing in our homes and marriages are not fundamentally tied to our personalities, worldviews, or backgrounds. They come from giving the garden over to the Devil and allowing him to take advantage of our lack of spiritual covering and authority by exploiting our personalities, worldviews, and backgrounds.

One final thought on this passage. A man doesn't have *absolute* authority over a woman. She is to come under him only as his authority aligns underneath the lordship of Christ. In other words, a husband cannot ask or require his wife to do something that violates a divine mandate in Scripture.

Because of the Angels

Again, when you are living out of alignment, you're living under the consequences of the curse, and you've lost your capacity to rule. When you are in alignment, you are living under the blessing and have regained your rule. So the question regarding your marriage is not so much whether he (or she) annoys you, or whether you disagree about certain things; it's whether or not you want to rule your world or lose that rule. It's up to you because God has established a certain positional framework within which we all must abide. And He has done it for a purpose.

This often-overlooked purpose for hierarchy is found in 1 Corinthians 11. Paul began this passage by talking about a woman's hair as her covering, since she is the glory of a man, and he also talked about a man being the glory of God (verses 4–7). Paul reminds us after this that the woman originated from the man and was created for the man's sake, but neither is independent of the other, since the man is now birthed from the woman (verses 8–9, 11–12). Sandwiched in between these statements is found the reason behind Paul's emphasis on a symbolic covering that represents the covering of headship: "Therefore the woman ought to have a symbol of authority on her head, *because of the angels*" (verse 10).

What does "because of the angels" mean? The Devil is an angel. His name was Lucifer. God created Lucifer to be the archangel. He was an angel of incredible glory, as well as unparalleled power and strength. There was only one caveat to Lucifer's control: It needed to come underneath God's order. But Lucifer didn't like that. He wanted to be equal to God, to be like the Most High, and he didn't want to have to answer to anyone. In fact, he wanted everyone to have to answer to him.

Lucifer didn't like God's prescribed order; he wanted to run his own show. So Lucifer rebelled. He found those who would follow him, and he sought to take a place above God Himself. Yet when he rebelled, he was cursed, and a third of the angels, those who rebelled with him, were also cursed. They were placed on planet earth, which served as a holding cell until the time God set for their eternal destruction.

In the meantime, God created man—Adam—and from Adam He created Eve. When Lucifer tempted Adam and Eve to also break the divine order, he turned their blessing and rule into a curse. In other words, they got cursed because of an angel. Satan, an angel turned bad, brought about pain in employment, pain in finances, pain in childbirth, pain in the ground, and pain in families.

In other words, angels aren't just sitting around doing nothing. They are either supporting the divine order (God's angels) or seeking to twist it with another order (Satan's followers). Angels are very involved in our lives and marriages. The good angels we call angels; the bad ones we call demons. Demons seek to take their own spirit of rebellion and create chaos in our homes by playing on differences in personalities, desires, and weaknesses. When we give in to these differences in our marriages and place ourselves outside our lanes—men in the lane of God and His rule, and women in the lane of men as their final authority—we lose the capacity to rule our homes, our children, our careers, and more.

> ❖❖❖❖❖
>
> *When Lucifer tempted Adam and Eve to also break the divine order, he turned their blessing and rule into a curse.*
>
> ❖❖❖❖❖

Ephesians 3:10 states, ". . . so that the manifold wisdom of God might now be made known through the church to the rulers and the authorities in the heavenly places." The angels are waiting for their instructions by looking at how you and I as members of the body of Christ—the church—choose to operate. When we are operating correctly, there is a signal to the angels to bring God's will to bear on earth. When we are operating out of alignment, the doors are open and the signal is given for the demons to bring even greater chaos.

Angels are available to all of us to provide protection, guidance, and more. But a lot of our angels are taking a break because they don't see the order that grants them permission to enter our world and invoke our rule. If you're not in order, in alignment, then the angels won't move, because that's what got the first group cast out of heaven to begin with—operating out of order.

When Jesus called Nathanael to follow him, Jesus told him that He saw Nathanael sitting under a fig tree. Because of this, Nathanael believed that Jesus was the Son of God. But Jesus told him that he would see even greater things than these: "Truly, truly, I say to you, you will see the heavens opened and the angels of God ascending and descending on the Son of Man" (John 1:51).

As a couple, you can regain your right to rule and exercise the dominion God has called you to live out.

Jesus was sharing the image of a ladder coming down out of heaven bringing God's rule—"Your kingdom come. Your will be done" (Matthew 6:10)—from heaven to earth. This is similar to the ladder Jacob saw at Bethel, where he witnessed the angels descending from and ascending to heaven (Genesis 28:12).

The reason many of us aren't witnessing God's hand of intervention, favor, and blessing in our marriages is because we are limiting positive angelic involvement. Our ladders are strewn across our yards—lying flat or leaning up against the wrong walls. Order is critical because it reveals a heart of obedience and trust. Disorder embodies rebellion and pride.

As a couple, you can regain your right to rule and exercise the dominion God has called you to live out. You can get back your power, your answered prayers, and the blessings God has in store for you if you will both align yourselves in the right order under Him.

3

✤✤✤✤✤

OPPOSITION

A HEALTHY, VIBRANT MARRIAGE is all about focus. Is your focus on God and His purpose and power, or is it on yourself and what you want? A couple came to my office for counseling not too long ago, and they brought a list with them. This list must have had at least thirty or more things written on it. I remember feeling instantly depressed as I watched them pull out that list. It was as if I was a balloon, and someone had taken a needle and deflated me. *How am I going to help them solve so many issues?* I thought as they began to read each and every item on the list.

——— ✤✤✤✤✤ ———

A healthy, vibrant marriage is all about focus.

——— ✤✤✤✤✤ ———

On and on they read, naming what sounded like legitimate sources of conflict. These were real issues, and I could see why they were not getting along. Once the couple finished reading the list, the husband handed it to me. In a split second, I had to make a decision. Was I going to go through this list with them and provide input on each issue they'd written down, or was I going to address the source of their conflict?

I looked at the list. Then I looked at the couple, both of whom had hopelessness and even anger written all over their faces. Then I looked back at the list, carefully and thoughtfully penned. And I tore it up. Right there in front of them. You can imagine what their faces looked like then. They had taken quite a bit of time to prepare this list for our meeting, and I had just shredded it.

I leaned toward them and said in a soft but firm tone, "What you just gave me is the fruit. It's real, but it's the fruit. It's like a firecracker that shoots up into the sky and explodes. Only one thing is shot up there, but when it explodes, it goes into all of these other directions. What I want to talk to you about is the 'one thing,' not the explosion.

"We could talk about these thirty things on your list, but nothing will ultimately change in your marriage, because this one thing is missing: the spiritual foundation of your relationship. Without establishing and maintaining a solid spiritual relationship, your list of thirty things, once solved, will just morph into another thirty, and you'll wind up back in here the same time next year with another list of thirty things to solve."

> *What makes a marriage strong is loving with a biblical love grounded in patience, kindness, loyalty, grace, and more, which is in alignment with God's covenantal purpose for marriage.*

I could tell they were both listening intently, so I continued. "Get this one thing right, and all the other things will fall into place. Get a divine perspective on your marriage as the foundation for your home, and you'll discover who your true enemy is—and it is not each other."

When we fight in our marriages, we assume that our spouses are the problem. And that's exactly what the Devil wants. He wants you to believe that your spouse is the problem—not you. He knows you will never fix the real problem if you believe that the person you are fighting with is the problem. But your spouse is not the problem. The problem is a spiritual one brought on by your own sinful flesh or by a rebellious and clever enemy of God.

Think about it: Much of what you end up fighting about in your marriage has nothing to do with what you are really fighting about, does it? There's something deeper—an unmet need, a lack of trust, a lack of respect, or any number of other things. These are the root of the problem and the fights. However, what makes a marriage strong is loving with a biblical love grounded in patience, kindness, loyalty, grace, and more, which is in alignment with God's covenantal purpose for marriage.

Yet a lot of the things we end up fighting about have to do with the consequences of our own choices, as well as the demonic realm working against us. One little thing can easily turn into a conflict that puts us on a path to divorce court. And we end up wondering how something so small could destroy something so big.

It can do that because, again, it's not that one little thing. It's about breaking the marriage covenant through a lack of submission (by both parties) under the transcendence of God, a lack of alignment with each other and God, or violating the covenantal rules of love and respect.

It's like asking how one small piece of fruit in the garden of Eden could have caused so much pain. It caused so much pain for all future generations because it wasn't just about a piece of fruit. It was about the effect: the curse, which came from the cause, which was disobedience to God's rule.

If you are unable to truly comprehend and correct your focus by making a spiritual connection to everything that goes on in your marriage, you will continue to rant and rave about whatever the current issue is. You will continue to focus on the thing that's happening without realizing that the core issue is to blame: a failure to align under the fundamentals of a covenant in order to be in a position to receive the blessings God has promised. After all, isn't that what happened to Adam and Eve in the garden?

Again, it really wasn't about the fruit, was it? Rather, it was a failure to abide by God's covenantal provisions. It was a failure to take God at His Word. Once God's Word begins to get twisted and warped, all hell breaks loose. We witnessed that not only with Adam and Eve but also with their children, when Cain went on to kill Abel. Adam and Eve's marriage eventually affected the entire world, as God ultimately destroyed it in a flood. Even to this day, we live under the curse of what they did in the garden.

Satan showed up to get Adam and Eve to do more than simply take a bite out of some fruit. He showed up to destroy the family so that he could regain a portion of the rule he lost at his fall. Satan showed up to distort God's image, since male and female were created in the image of God and together were the most complete manifestation of God's image. He did this by challenging and changing God's Word, reversing the roles of men and women, and introducing a demonic presence into their life decisions. Satan wants to destroy your marriage not just because he wants to destroy your marriage but because he knows that in doing so, he'll also destroy your legacy. He'll mess up the future of your children and their children. Whoever owns the family owns the future. The best way for Satan to get to the family is to target your marriage. That's why he approached Eve in the garden the way he did, seeking to subtly turn her heart and her mind from God.

———— ✤✤✤✤✤ ————

Satan wants to destroy your marriage because he knows that in doing so, he'll also destroy your legacy.

———— ✤✤✤✤✤ ————

God is referenced in a distinct way in Scripture regarding His relationship with humanity before Satan appeared to Eve and tempted her to eat of the forbidden fruit. Every time God is spoken of in conjunction with Adam, He is called "the LORD God." Whenever we read the word "LORD" written in all caps, it stands for the name of God, which is translated from the word *Yahweh*. This name in the original language reflects God's character and covenantal relationship as "master and absolute ruler."

However, when Satan approached Eve to persuade her to do that which she shouldn't do, Satan didn't refer to God the way God referred to Himself. Rather, Satan removed the name "LORD" altogether and simply said, "Indeed, has God said . . . ?" (Genesis 3:1). In this subtle reduction of terms, Satan sought to strip from the conversation any association with God's rulership over and relationship with humanity. In doing so, he kept the concept of religion intact. After all, he did say "God." But he removed the relational element of divine authority. Satan chose to bypass Adam and approach Eve in a way that would get her to believe that the authority was actually hers to have. In addition, the Evil One spoke to Eve only about the good that the Tree of Knowledge had to offer, not the evil that would result from it. Satan is good at giving only half the story.

In biting the fruit that had been forbidden by the One who had the right to forbid it, both Adam and Eve changed their view of their creator from that of "LORD God" to "God." This then ended the intimate fellowship with Him that they had once shared, and it also ended the freedom of intimacy they had once shared with each other. Not only that, but it pruned the power of their dominion, which had flowed to and through them from the ultimate Ruler.

The primary reason Satan stirs up conflict in our marital relationships is because he wants to flip the rulership in our lives. He is seeking to dethrone the one true King, who reigns over both partners in a marriage, and then Satan wants to offer each partner the misguided notion that he or she has the wisdom and the ability to live apart from God. As we learned from Adam and Eve, and as I'm sure you can testify in your own life and marriage, decisions made apart from God's wisdom notoriously wind up causing more harm than good.

Decisions made apart from God's wisdom notoriously wind up causing more harm than good.

When Satan is allowed to stoke the fires of discontent and contempt in our homes, he distorts the image of God through us as married couples and keeps us from accomplishing our own dominion purposes. Essentially, when you view your spouse as your enemy and fail to recognize the true enemy, Satan, you are getting hoodwinked. Satan is playing the end against the middle to limit your ability to carry out all that God desires to do in and through both of you. When you don't see your enemy for who he is—a clever manipulator and deceiver who knows just the right buttons to push to turn you against each other—you will forever be reacting to your spouse rather than recognizing that Satan is just the vehicle to stop what God is trying to do.

By destroying your marriage, Satan destroys the future of your family and negatively impacts society at large. That's why you must commit your marriage to prayer and cultivate a real relationship in humility while seeking God's wisdom and guidance and asking for His love, grace, and mercy in all things.

I'm happy to say that when the couple I mentioned earlier with the long list of issues sought to view each other and their relationship through the lens of God's purposes, they made every attempt to cultivate and keep that which they were given. Over time I literally saw the wife's countenance lift as if she were becoming a brand-new woman. I also saw the husband enjoy a relationship with his wife that used to bring him dread. To this day they are living out the fullness of a life together, in the grace and knowledge of the Lord Jesus Christ.

Identify Your True Enemy

A number of years ago, a well-known football player named Conrad Dobler was featured in a popular Miller Lite television commercial. Perhaps you remember it; in a matter of a few seconds, he managed to incite a near riot among a group of spectators. At his urging, one side claimed, "Tastes great!" "Less filling!" the other retorted.

As the controversy was about to turn into a fight, the camera cut to Dobler, who was sneaking out a back exit. Believe it or not, this tongue-in-cheek tactic concocted by Madison Avenue to sell beer is a vital spiritual lesson for marriage: *It's important to identify your true enemy.*

The fans in the bleachers thought their opponents were those who disagreed with them. In truth, the entire audience had only one enemy: Conrad Dobler.

The whole of the universe is divided into two rival kingdoms. The first is the kingdom of light or righteousness, ruled by God. The other is the kingdom of darkness or evil, commanded by Satan. He is our enemy—our only enemy—and our world is the battleground where his efforts to compete with God are played out. "For our struggle is not against flesh and blood, but against the rulers, against the powers, against the world forces of this darkness, against the spiritual forces of wickedness in the heavenly places" (Ephesians 6:12).

Calvary was the definitive blow that sealed the Devil's fate. When Jesus Christ died on the cross, a cataclysmic thing happened: Satan was soundly and completely defeated.

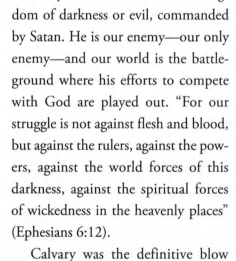

Calvary was the definitive blow that sealed the Devil's fate. When Jesus Christ died on the cross, a cataclysmic thing happened: Satan was soundly and completely defeated. He was beaten beyond hope of recovery, and he knew it. You may ask, "Tony, if Satan is defeated, how come he is still disrupting my marriage? Why are there problems we can't overcome and challenges we can't face? If the Enemy has been so soundly defeated, why is he still so powerful?"

Satan has been defeated. But like a person beaten in life, he doesn't want to go down alone. As chaplain for the Dallas Mavericks, I've definitely seen some basketball in my day. During a recent season, the Mavericks missed the play-offs by a country mile. They were defeated long before the season ended. Still, during their final game, they played with a passion for victory. Why? Because dealing a late-season loss to a rival team would affect that team's chances of becoming champions.

In other words, "We may not be going to the play-offs, but neither are you!" In the sports world, that's the way the game is played. Marriage is no different when it comes to Satan. He's no longer looking to win the final victory, but if he can defeat and disable you to prevent you from achieving yours, he will have accomplished his goal. Satan's goal for you and your spouse is to rob you of your own spiritual championship bid and drag you down to his defeatist level. If you're saved, he can't drag either of you into hell, but he can try to render you ineffective and miserable on earth.

Satan knows what the apostle Paul knew, that God has "blessed us with every spiritual blessing in the heavenly places in Christ" (Ephesians 1:3). The Devil understands your

> *We will never know God's power if there is no temptation. We will never know His strength if there is no opportunity to use His armor.*

potential individually and as a couple under the Dominion Covenant. He wants to revoke your rule so that God's name won't be glorified and God's kingdom won't be advanced on earth. Satan is committed to seeing to it that you never reach your potential.

One of the reasons God allows hell to be hell on earth and the Devil to wage war is so that each of us can know God's name and recognize the power that comes from Him. Because we will never know His name if there is no war. We will never know His power if there is no temptation. We will never know His strength if there is no opportunity to use His armor. So He lets the war rage on, often in ways that cause us to get on our knees and seek Him so that we will grow closer to Him.

The Enemy's Strategy

Satan is most effective when he works secretly, behind the scenes. Like Conrad Dobler in the commercial I mentioned earlier, Satan would prefer that others get the credit for his work. In fact, Satan would be perfectly happy to convince you that he doesn't exist and that your true problem is your spouse. That's why most of his attacks seem to come from other sources, most notably from the person you married.

Do you think at times that your marriage would be wonderful if it were not for your spouse? Most of the problems in marriage can be traced to relational issues. You may think that your mate is making your life miserable. Or perhaps you think your children or your coworkers are causing friction in your marriage.

But look closer, and you're bound to see Satan behind the scenes pulling the strings and pushing the buttons. He uses people to engineer your spiritual downfall by driving wedges between you and your spouse that shatter your unity and draw your focus away from God.

The Christian life is like wood in a fireplace. Try lighting a single log, and you will find out that it won't burn for long. Logs burn best in the presence of other logs. In the same way, your ability to remain spiritually on fire is a function of your relationships with the other "logs" in your life and how closely you relate to them. Your ability as a couple to remain spiritually strong is a function of your relationship with each other before the Lord. How often do you pray together? It should be daily.

How often do you pray for your marriage? Again, it should be daily, if not several times throughout the day. Do you worship together? Go to church together? Talk about the messages together? Read God's Word together? I understand that life is busy, but if you want the ability to go through this life together "till death do us part," then the spiritual component of life must be an integral part of who you are as a couple.

God supplies the strength we need to successfully do battle with the Devil. That may seem obvious. But judging from the way we treat this truth, it bears repeating: "Be strong in the Lord and in the strength of His might. Put on the full armor of God, so that you will be able to stand firm against the schemes of the devil" (Ephesians 6:10–11).

Many of us tend to swing toward one of two extremes when it comes to the Devil. Some overestimate him. They become fearful and timid, lest Satan leap on them. Remember, "greater is He who is in you than he who is in the world" (1 John 4:4). Others underestimate the Devil. Yes, Satan is a defeated foe. But even though he is nothing more than a condemned death-row inmate awaiting execution, it is not wise to sleep in his cell.

Notice that in our text, the apostle Paul tells us to be strong in the Lord. In our humanity, we haven't the power to overcome angels, even fallen ones like the Devil and his legions. Psalm 8:4–5 (KJV) makes it clear that God created us a little lower than the angels.

The bottom line is this: You can't beat the Devil on your own. God Himself is the only one capable of putting the Devil in his place, and that's exactly what He'll do someday. (That place is described for us in Revelation 20.) In the meantime, the Lord limits Satan's reach. In addition, He empowers us to achieve victory in our day-to-day encounters with darkness.

In Acts 19:13–17, we read about some nonbelieving Jewish exorcists who decided to try expelling demons by magically chanting the name of Jesus. "I adjure you by Jesus whom Paul preaches," they'd say. And one day a spirit answered them, "I recognize Jesus, and I know about Paul, but who are you?" The spirit leaped on them, thrashed them soundly, and sent them away stripped and wounded. Jesus's name is not a magic formula, though some people have used it that way over the years. Paul's strength and ours is the product of an abiding, growing personal intimacy with the Lord, not some high-sounding chant or incantation. Recall that the people called on "Jesus whom Paul preaches."

Victory in your marriage requires your personal relationship with Jesus Christ to be close, not piggybacked on someone else's. That's a surefire pathway to defeat if you have to borrow from the faith of another to fight for your marriage. Your strength is not accumulated or earned. It is supplied by the

> ❖ ❖ ❖ ❖ ❖
>
> *Victory in your marriage requires your personal relationship with Jesus Christ to be close, not piggybacked on someone else's.*
>
> ❖ ❖ ❖ ❖ ❖

grace of God, who equips you to live the life to which He has called you, but it is accessed through direct communion with Him.

The apostle Paul wrote,

Though we walk in the flesh, we do not war according to the flesh, for the weapons of our warfare are not of the flesh, but divinely powerful for the destruction of fortresses. (2 Corinthians 10:3–4)

Doing battle with Satan in your home requires more than a New Year's resolution and a dose of willpower. Spiritual warfare requires spiritual weaponry, such as those items described for us in Ephesians 6:13–17. I discuss spiritual warfare in more depth in a book on that subject titled *Victory in Spiritual Warfare*, but let's touch briefly on it here.

I can envision Paul in a prison cell dictating his letter to the Ephesian church. Perhaps he paused, searching for a proper illustration to help him communicate this vital truth. Suddenly his gaze fell on the Roman centurion to whom he was chained. Noticing the various components of the guard's uniform, Paul set about to describe six vital pieces of armor considered "standard issue" in God's army:

Take up the full armor of God, so that you will be able to resist in the evil day, and having done everything, to stand firm. Stand firm therefore, having girded your loins with truth, and having put on the breastplate of righteousness, and having shod your feet with the preparation of the gospel of peace; in additional to all, taking up the shield of faith with which you will be able to extinguish all the flaming arrows of the evil one. And take the helmet of salvation, and the sword of the Spirit, which is the word of God. (verses 13–17)

You will experience the victory that is yours for the taking only when you put on and use the full armor of God. God makes these battle instruments available to you, but He won't force you to wear them or take them up. He won't have faith for you. He won't lift your shield for you. He won't force peace, truth, or righteousness on you. In your marriage and your life, you must do battle God's way, with His armor, against an enemy who is seeking daily, even hourly, to take you down.

A young boy once went to the zoo with his dad. As they passed by the lions' den, one of the lions let out a ferocious roar. Startled, the young boy grabbed on to his father, covered his face, and began to cry. His father asked him, "What's wrong?"

The young boy replied, "Don't you see the lion?"

"Yes," his father answered, "but I also see the cage."

Married couple, Satan is a defeated foe. He is a caged lion. Victory in your marriage must rest on the reality that God has given you everything that you need to live in light of this truth in order to experience all that He has planned for you and become all He created you to be. But God won't dress you. You have to put on the armor of God every day in order to experience the victory that is yours.

4

❖❖❖❖❖

OATHS

HAVE YOU EVER WONDERED why so much of the Bible is taken up with the issue of covenants? In Genesis 8–9, God made a covenant with Noah after the great flood, promising that He would never again destroy the earth. In Genesis 12, God made a covenant with Abram promising to provide him with a seed—a son—who would be a blessing to the nations. In Exodus 19–24, God entered into a covenant with the Israelites at Mount Sinai after their release from bondage in Egypt.

God also entered into a covenant with King David, promising him that He would build a house for him and establish his throne forever (2 Samuel 7). There was also a new covenant—first promised in Jeremiah 31:31 but then fulfilled in Jesus, who ratified the new covenant with His blood shed on the cross (Luke 22:20). In fact, the idea of the old covenant with Israel and the new covenant of Christ set the major divisions of the Bible into the Old and New Testaments.

Why is the Bible so preoccupied with the theme of covenants, and what does that have to do with your marriage? Let me answer the Bible question first, and then I'll tie it in to your marriage.

The main reason the concept of covenants is such a prevalent theme in the Bible is that a covenant is the means by which God administers or governs His kingdom. Marriage is a supreme covenantal union designed by God to allow both partners to fully maximize their potential in Christ. If we want to understand how to make the most of our marriages under God's rule, then we need to understand how covenants work and, in particular, how they relate to marriage.

What Is a Covenant?

Before we approach the tangible link between covenants and the health and vitality of your marriage, I want to give a brief overview of biblical covenants. This will provide the context for greater awareness of the preeminence that the marital covenant ought to have. In the Bible, a covenant is a divinely created bond. It is a "spiritually binding relationship between God and His people inclusive of certain agreements, conditions, benefits, responsibilities, and effects." God's power, provision, and authority in relation to His people operate under His covenants. Whenever God wanted to formalize His relationship with His people, He would establish a covenant.

> *Marriage is a supreme covenantal union designed by God to allow both partners to fully maximize their potential in Christ.*

A covenant involves far more than a contract. In a biblical covenant, you do more than enter a business partnership. Rather, you enter into an intimate relationship with the other person or persons in the covenant. This is the first of three distinctions that set a covenant apart from a contract.

When God entered into a covenant with the people of Israel, the language used was that of mutual love and concern (Deuteronomy 6:4–5), much like the language a husband and wife use when entering into a marriage covenant. Jesus's new covenant also exemplified this quality of relationship between God and humankind.

The second distinction between a covenant and a contract is that covenants in the Bible were designed to bring blessings to the parties involved in the relationship. For example, in Deuteronomy 29:9, Moses warned the Israelites to keep God's covenant for that reason: "So keep the words of this covenant to do them, that you may prosper in all that you do." When Moses spoke of prospering in all the people would do, it implied more than just material gain but included what Christ came to secure for us: abundant life (John 10:10).

The third distinction between a covenant and a contract is that covenants are ratified in blood. For example, God took His relational commitment to bless Israel so seriously that He sealed the covenant in blood by offering a sacrifice (Exodus 29:16–46). God also made a covenant with Abram in Genesis 15 and 17, reaffirming His promise to give Abram a son. In Genesis 17, we find the relationship of the covenant to blood, and in fact, this blood ratification became an ongoing ritual affirming membership in God's covenant of blessing from then on.

Covenants are serious matters, and their ratification through blood indicates the lengths to which God will go to establish and keep His covenants with His people. In marriage, when two partners come together as sexual virgins and engage in sex on their wedding night, God has so designed the woman that she bleeds in this first encounter, thus ratifying the covenant of marriage.

> *Covenants are serious matters, and their ratification through blood indicates the lengths to which God will go to establish and keep His covenants with His people.*

Another way to understand a covenant is through its synonym *covering*. If and when you operate under God's covenant, you are operating under His covering. Consider this analogy: When it is raining outside, most people will open an umbrella. The umbrella covers them from the rain. The umbrella doesn't stop the rain, but it does stop the rain from reaching them. It doesn't change what is happening around a person, but it does change what happens to him or her.

Living under God's covering may not change the challenges you face in your marriage, but under His covering, those challenges won't affect you—cause you to react, worry, or argue—at the level they normally would if you were out from under His covering. That's why it is so critical for spouses to understand the covenantal design of marriage. The marriage vows are a serious set of vows that bring with them either blessing or cursing, depending upon how those vows are honored or dismissed.

The covering of the covenant is a lot like the armor of God that Paul spoke about in Ephesians 6. The armor is there to protect you, but God will never force you to wear it. He's not going to stick the shield of faith in your hand; you have to pick it up. It's there if you need it, but it's up to you whether you use it rightly. Similarly, if it's raining and you have an umbrella but don't use it, you'll get wet. You have to make the choice.

To fully benefit from God's covering—His power, provision, authority, peace, and blessing—you must not only be *in* His covenant; you must align yourself *under* His covenantal rule in your marriage. But first you must understand five of the characteristics that define a covenant created by God.

1. *Transcendence.* This refers to God being in charge. You may be more familiar with the term *sovereignty*, which means the same thing. God is distinct. He is not a part of His creation. Rather, He is separate from it. He sits above it and outside of it. Covenants are both initiated and ruled by God. The first thing we must understand to function properly under God's covenant—in particular, His covenant of marriage—is that He is in charge. We must decide whether to pray "My will be done" in our marriages or "Thy will be done." This is why God says that man should not be allowed to put asunder what God has joined together.

> *The first thing we must understand to function properly under God's covenant—in particular, His covenant of marriage—is that He is in charge.*

2. *Hierarchy.* God's covenants are administered through a chain of command, or hierarchy, that functions under His ultimate authority. We looked at 1 Corinthians 11:3 earlier, but it makes the point here as well. In this passage, Paul stated, "I want you to understand that Christ is the head of every man, and the man is the head of a woman, and God is the head of Christ." This means that everyone in God's kingdom functions under authority—under a "head." This extends even to the life of the

Trinity, where Christ is obedient to the Father's commands in order to accomplish His plan of redemption for our world.

The blessings that flow from being in a covenantal relationship with God flow through this chain of command. In fact, 1 Corinthians 7:14 highlights the lengths to which this hierarchy goes in allowing God's blessings to flow to a spouse: "For the unbelieving husband is sanctified through his wife, and the unbelieving wife is sanctified through her believing husband; for otherwise your children are unclean, but now they are holy."

This oath outlines the blessings for obedience and the curses for disobedience that are binding upon the covenant partner.

3. *Ethics.* God's covenants contain specific rules (or ethics), stipulations, and guidelines that govern the relationship of blessing with the covenant partners. Let's look again at the first marriage. When God placed Adam in the garden of Eden, He framed His relationship with Adam by establishing a specific rule: You must not eat from the Tree of the Knowledge of Good and Evil. Covenants function by a cause-and-effect rule. If Adam (and Eve) had obeyed God's command, he would have experienced the full blessing of living in the garden, but when he broke this command (with Eve), he was banned from the garden. Adam and Eve had to decide whether to submit to divine rule or rely on human reason, and that decision determined the direction their lives and marriage would take. Obedience or disobedience to God's revealed Word was the key to a heavenly or hellish relationship.

This was no less true for the people of Israel in their covenant with God. Joshua, the leader of Israel after Moses, was commanded to "be careful to do according to all the law which Moses My servant commanded you; do not turn from it to the right or to the left, so that you may have success wherever you go" (Joshua 1:7).

4. *Sanctions.* God's covenants also contain an oath, a sanction, or a pledge that the covenant partner must make. This oath outlines the blessings for obedience and the curses for disobedience that are binding upon the covenant partner. The clearest example of this is in Deuteronomy 27–30, where Moses

read to the Israelites the list of blessings and curses that were attached to God's covenant with His people. Moses closed out the list with a final warning to the people, saying, "I have set before you life and death, the blessing and the curse. So choose life" (30:19).

5. *Inheritance.* Each of God's covenants also contains long-term repercussions or generational inheritance implications for obedience and disobedience. Israel was warned that their disobedience to the Ten Commandments would result in their penalty being passed on to "the third and the fourth generations of those who hate Me" (Exodus 20:5). As such, we should always be aware that the consequences of our decisions in our marriages not only affect us and our spouses, but they can ultimately affect our children, their children, and any others within our sphere of influence, which is what we are experiencing today in the devolution of the culture.

Renewing Your Vows

When you got married, you entered into a spiritually and legally binding vow. The ceremonial vow you made to each other is the public display of your marriage covenant before God. This can be compared to the act of baptism when you entered into the new covenant of salvation with Jesus Christ.

Both of these vows have a follow-up action that points back to this agreement. For both baptism and salvation, the action of remembering the vow is what we call Communion. Sexual intimacy, like Communion, is revisiting the vow made at the time of marriage, declaring that two individuals were now united as one flesh.

Sexual intimacy is far more important and far more powerful than many of us realize. It is to marriage what Communion is to the Cross: revisiting the foundational oath of the covenant. Sexual intimacy in marriage is usually understood only in terms of its physical dimension. Not that the physical part of sex isn't wonderful—it is! But why stop there? Sexual intimacy is a powerful force to enrich your life not only physically but also spiritually. Sexual intimacy not only revisits the vow in a marriage relationship, but it is the ongoing expression of commitment, tenderness, and passion. One of the worst things you can do is to make ritual what was designed to be sacred. Don't ever allow sexual intimacy, something so completely profound, to turn into something ordinary.

I'm amazed at how many couples I counsel struggle in the area of sexuality. Either their sex lives have become so dormant that nothing is there, or there has been sexual abandonment or immorality by one of the partners. Precious little negatively affects a marriage as much as deviation from what God designed sex to be within it. Unfortunately, I believe much of this happens simply because spouses don't honor or view sexual relations through the lens of the covenantal renewal of their vows.

Sexual intimacy not only revisits the vow in a marriage relationship, but it is the ongoing expression of commitment, tenderness, and passion.

This can be compared to the frustration the apostle Paul expressed to the church at Corinth. The believers there had begun to misuse the Communion table and, as a result, were suffering the consequences of their actions (1 Corinthians 11:27–32). The same thing is happening in many marriages today because the meaning of sex has become so warped that it has lost its value, and couples are suffering the resulting consequences.

God doesn't take covenants or the things symbolically attached to them lightly. As we've been introduced to God's covenantal structure and purpose, we've seen how this legally binding vow includes effects in our lives and the lives of those around us with regard to God's involvement. Consider this most-revealing passage in Malachi:

> This is another thing you do: you cover the altar of the LORD with tears, with weeping and with groaning, because He no longer regards the offering or accepts it with favor from your hand. Yet you say, "For what reason?" Because the LORD has been a witness between you and the wife of your youth, against whom you have dealt treacherously, though she is your companion and your wife by covenant. But not one has done so who has a remnant of the Spirit. And what did that one do while he was seeking a godly offspring? Take heed then to

your spirit, and let no one deal treacherously against the wife of your youth. (2:13–15)

The words you exchanged on your wedding day when you promised to love, honor, and cherish each other were not just part of the ceremony. They were said in the context of making your relationship a legally binding covenant under the principle of two becoming one flesh (Mark 10:6–8). God takes marriage vows so seriously that in Malachi, He told His people that He wasn't going to receive their worship because they were breaking those vows. Imagine how offended God must have been to refuse the worship of those He created in His image for the specific purpose of worshipping Him. That's how critical it is to honor the covenant of marriage.

It Takes Three

As I've said before, marriage is a sacred covenant, not just a social contract. It consists of more than a relationship arranged for the purpose of procreation or even companionship. Marriage provides a unique covenantal environment in which you have an even greater opportunity to live out your destiny both individually and as a couple.

The book of Ecclesiastes is filled with powerful wisdom and insightful truths, such as this principle: "A cord of three strands is not quickly torn apart" (4:12). This is an important key to a successful marriage. When two people enter into a covenant, they enter into it along with a third person, God. Just as the Trinity is made up of three persons who are one—God the Father, God the Son, and God the Holy Spirit—marriage is an earthly replica of this divine Trinity—the husband, the wife, and God.

God is the cord that not only keeps you together but also keeps you strong and able to do all He has designed for you to do and enjoy.

You cannot leave God at the altar and expect to have a thriving marriage. God must join you in your home. When He does, and when you align yourself within the parameters of love, respect, commitment, and compassion He has established, He can do marvels with your marriage. You cannot do it alone. You cannot even do it as husband and wife. God is the cord that not only keeps you together but also keeps you strong and able to do all He has designed for you to do and enjoy.

God's power is best freed to flow when you recognize and respect the marital covenant as a covenant, not merely as a convenient companionship you entered into. When Christ arose from the dead, He gave humankind access to the power of His resurrection (Romans 6:4; Philippians 3:10) and the presence of the Holy Spirit (John 14:16–18). That power can enable you and your mate to live together, love each other, trust each other, and share life with each other until death parts you.

God made marriage, and because He did, He knows just what you need to make yours not only survive but also thrive. Commit yourselves to Him by functioning within the parameters of His divinely orchestrated covenant of marriage. As you do, He will strengthen your marriage into something that He can use not only to glorify Himself but to bring you and your spouse fulfillment, purpose, and pleasure.

It Also Takes One

In Genesis 2:24, we read, "Therefore [because Eve was taken out of man] shall a man leave his father and his mother [Adam didn't have parents but would have left them for Eve], and shall cleave unto his wife: and they shall be one flesh" (KJV).

That verse summarizes what a marriage relationship is to consist of: leaving, cleaving, and becoming one. Not only does it take three to make a marriage; it also takes two spouses uniting as a single unit—husband and wife. It is a great tragedy that although most people have heard these words many times, they don't know what true oneness is.

Marriage is not a solo; it is a duet playing the same song.

I'll go into this in more detail in the next chapter, but just to introduce it now, oneness doesn't mean sameness. Oneness means working together toward the same goal. People working together toward the same goal will have to, out of necessity, communicate, cooperate, and merge strengths with strengths while overlooking or overcoming each other's weaknesses. You are on your spouse's team. The stronger the two of you are together, the stronger you will be as individuals. This not only requires time; it requires an authentic commitment. Marriage is not a solo; it is a duet playing the same song.

Ladies, even if a man says that he loves you, and as much as you'd like to think that he's promising to share his whole life with you, he may only be planning to work you into his schedule. He may not be planning to cut back on any activities or give up anything for you. That kind of man doesn't know what marriage is about.

God specifically asked men to give up the closest ties they have in order to honor their wives: "Therefore a man *leaves* his father and mother and *embraces* his wife" (Genesis 2:24, MSG). Since one of a woman's greatest needs in marriage is to feel secure, a husband must make that a priority.

Marriage is a covenantal union designed to strengthen the ability of each partner to carry out God's plan in their lives. Again, marriage takes two individuals and makes them even stronger together as one.

5

✤✤✤✤✤✤

ONENESS

AT THE HEART of the first marriage recorded for us in Genesis 2 is the principle of oneness, also known as unity. This is because God's own nature is comprised of oneness, along with the diversity of the Trinity. It's also because God's kingdom purposes are realized only in a context of unity, which is why Jesus said in Matthew 12:25 that "any kingdom divided against itself is laid waste; and any city or house divided against itself will not stand."

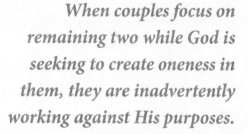

When couples focus on remaining two while God is seeking to create oneness in them, they are inadvertently working against His purposes.

This is why it is such a high priority for the Evil One to bring discord and disharmony into homes and marriages. As I mentioned earlier, Satan seeks to divide, because whatever he can divide, he can conquer. Disunity keeps God at bay and His kingdom from being expanded. Likewise, it distorts the image of His glory.

When couples focus on remaining two while God is seeking to create oneness in them, they are inadvertently working against His purposes. The principle of unity must be understood and vigorously pursued if a marriage is to truly experience God's manifest presence.

Displayed on the official seal of the United States of America and on much of our national currency is the well-known Latin phrase *E pluribus unum* or "out of the many, one." The phrase came into use very early in the American Revolutionary War, because the key to gaining independence from Great Britain was in uniting the various American colonies to resist this foreign, oppressive government. This meant that people with different interests, political systems, and backgrounds had to find a way to join their efforts or be crushed by the superior military power of Great Britain.

At the signing of the Declaration of Independence, Benjamin Franklin famously remarked, "Gentlemen, we must now all hang together, or we shall most assuredly all hang separately." His words reflect this sentiment that unity must be forged out of a shared commitment to defeat a common enemy.

At the heart of our national story lies the issue of forming, in the words of the Preamble to the US Constitution, a "more perfect union," and the coinciding story of the powers and pressures that can either strengthen that unity or put it at risk. As we look around at what plagues our nation today, it is clear that we are sewn together with a very fragile thread that requires constant attention to protect and maintain that "more perfect union."

If the issue of our unity or oneness, according to Jesus, is so critical to our witness, what do infighting and divisions say about us to a watching world?

This is no less true in our marriages. The divisions, arguments, and conflicts that are so tragically common in our marriages have affected us all on one level or another.

In John 17:21, Jesus prayed for His disciples and for those who would follow them: "May [they] all be one; even as You, Father, are in Me and I in You, that they also may be in Us, so that the world may believe that You sent Me." If the issue of our unity or oneness, according to Jesus, is so critical to our witness, what do infighting and divisions say about us to a watching world? This area of unity is critically tied to our mission found in Matthew 6:33, and so we must be "diligent to preserve the unity of the Spirit in the bond of peace" (Ephesians 4:3).

Recognizing the Gauge

Let's look at the issue of oneness in Paul's letter to the church at Ephesus, so that we can encourage a spirit of unity in our marriages:

> Therefore I, the prisoner of the Lord, implore you to walk in a
> manner worthy of the calling with which you have been called, with
> all humility and gentleness, with patience, showing tolerance for
> *one* another in love, being diligent to preserve the unity of the Spirit
> in the bond of peace. There is *one* body and *one* Spirit, just as also
> you were called in *one* hope of your calling; *one* Lord, *one* faith, *one*
> baptism, *one* God and Father of all who is over all and through all
> and in all. (Ephesians 4:1–6)

The book of Ephesians opens with a series of reminders to believers of everything God accomplished through Christ in His life, death, and resurrection, and all the benefits that come to us in light of His work on our behalf. In Paul's words, God has "blessed us with every spiritual blessing in the heavenly places" (1:3), and He will continue in the coming ages to "show the surpassing riches of His grace in kindness toward us in Christ Jesus" (2:7).

Right at the end of this extended reminder (chapters 1–3) comes the challenge to the Ephesian believers to "preserve the unity of the Spirit in the bond of peace" (4:3). Paul put it strongly, imploring them to be "diligent" (4:3) to preserve this unity. In other words, in light of these many blessings, they had a job to do, and they needed to work hard at holding up this spirit of unity among themselves. So, what is this idea of unity and why was it so important to Paul? And by implication, why is it so important to us in our marriage relationships?

First, let's address the definition of *unity*. In the first six verses of Ephesians 4, the word *one* is used eight times. In fact, in the Greek the word *unity* that Paul used here is a variation of the word *one*. In its simplest form, then, unity is any group of people who are characterized by "oneness," a shared purpose, vision, or direction.

Perhaps I can best illustrate this idea of oneness by indicating what unity is not. As I stated in the previous chapter, unity, or oneness, is not uniformity or sameness. Unity doesn't mean being just like your mate. God's creative variety can be seen all around us. God created things with different shapes, colors, sizes, and styles. Yet all of it, according to Psalm 19:1, was set in place for the one purpose of testifying to the "glory of God." Unity is not uniformity but uniqueness moving toward a common goal.

In sports, unity doesn't mean that every player on the field or in the stadium is playing the same position. All the players have unique talents, skills, identities, and responsibilities, but the goal to which they're headed is the same. A basketball team may have different positions for the five players on the court, but the one goal they're shooting at is the same. In the kitchen, unity of ingredients produces a delicious meal, but that same meal would never be produced if each ingredient was exactly like the others.

This concept of oneness sounds very much like the prayer Jesus prayed in His last moments with His disciples: "May [they] all be one" (John 17:21). The oneness Jesus prayed for was modeled on the oneness of relationship between the Father and the Son. In fact, Jesus prayed that His disciples would enter into this very same relationship: "I in them and you in Me, that they may be perfected in unity, so that the world may know that You sent Me, and loved them, even as You have loved Me" (verse 23).

When God created the woman from the rib of the man, resulting in the creation of two separate people, he was simultaneously implanting the desire for these to reconnect in oneness in order to experience completeness. This oneness was uniquely designed to join masculinity and femininity together in order to mirror the image of God in a unified way. This is why any union outside of this heterosexual covenant design of marriage is an "alien bond" that distorts the image of God.

Note that Paul defined the unity we are called to as a relational oneness "of the Spirit" (Ephesians 4:3), not unity centered on an agenda, a process, or even a shared living space. That's because unity is not a position but a person—the Holy Spirit. It doesn't involve a twelve-step process but centers on a relationship of oneness with the living God because of Christ's work in and through the presence of the Holy Spirit. As Paul himself put it, "There is one body and one Spirit, just as also you were called in one hope of your calling; one Lord, one faith, one baptism, one God and Father of all who is over all and through all and in all" (verses 4–6).

This means that marital unity begins with the relational oneness we share because of God's work through His Holy Spirit. We come closest to unity in marriage when we not only allow the Spirit to do His work in us but also point to and celebrate that work in each other.

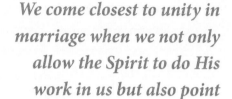

We come closest to unity in marriage when we not only allow the Spirit to do His work in us but also point to and celebrate that work in each other.

Unfortunately, some couples enter into marriage with a distorted view of unity, and their unrealistic expectations contribute to future disappointments. I see this at times when I perform wedding ceremonies. Often a portion of the ceremony includes two candles, which were lit prior to the ceremony and are then joined together to light an entirely new candle, thus symbolizing the unity of marriage. But it's a mistake when the bride and groom then blow out their individual candles.

I say this is a mistake because unless there is an intentional protection and respect for each other's unique identities, purposes, talents, skills, and callings, a couple is prone to fall prey to a marriage that consumes them rather than compels them both to greatness. When I meet with couples whose weddings I'm going to perform, I suggest that they don't blow out their individual candles after lighting a new, unified candle. Imagine attending a symphony where each musical instrument was a flute. It wouldn't be long before you would leave that symphony altogether. Rather, you hear beautiful music at a symphony because each unique instrument plays in harmony. That's what biblical unity in marriage ought to represent: the distinct lives of two individuals experiencing God's purpose for each of them in harmony with the other.

The Father didn't become the Son in order to be unified with Christ in the Trinity. The Holy Spirit didn't become the Father either. The reason the Trinity works so well in carrying out its various functions in our lives is because each member of the Trinity honors and respects the other and doesn't seek to become the other.

What I'm saying may seem out of place in a chapter specifically dedicated to oneness in marriage, but unless we understand and live out *true* unity in our marriages, we run the risk of cannibalizing each other not long after we say "I do." The healthiest marriages I've seen are those in which both parties maintain separate identities and purposes as they unite under the shared purpose of fulfilling the dominion rule of God in and through their partnership.

This understanding of unity offers each person in the marriage the opportunity to experience the maximum freedom that God intended for His creatures to enjoy. Within the boundaries of the marriage relationship, both the husband and wife are to fully pursue their calling under God—utilizing their giftedness to advance the potential of the other in an atmosphere of mutual trust and respect, so long as biblical priorities of the unity of the family are not being compromised (as illustrated by the Proverbs 31 excellent wife).

Many marriages *stifle* rather than *free* the partners to become all that God has called them to be. By inspiring nonbiblical, cultural, and religious standards and requirements, the full expression of kingdom authority that could be experienced by each partner in the marriage, as well as their collective impact, becomes limited. Kingdom marriage releases and expands—it doesn't restrict and limit—the legitimate dominion role of each spouse personally, as well as their impact together.

The freedom of individual uniqueness allows choice. Without personal choice and preference, a spouse can feel smothered or taken advantage of, or even lost altogether. One woman I counseled shared with me that she went with her husband and children to the library one day, and they each decided to pick out a book. They decided to go their separate ways, get one book each, and then meet back together to check out their books. As the kids ran off to their respective sections and her husband went off to his, the wife just stood there, paralyzed. For years her choices had been dictated by either the needs of her husband or those of her kids. Her preferences had been shaped by how she could please her family or become what they needed her to be at any given moment. Standing in the lobby of an enormous library with thousands of subjects to choose from, she didn't know which book she wanted to read just for her own enjoyment.

The movie *Runaway Bride*,[1] which came out in 1999, offers another example of losing your individuality in the act of blending with someone else. In this film the main character, Maggie, played by Julia Roberts, had a habit of darting whenever she walked down the aisle to get married. No one could figure out why, not even her, until late in the movie when she came to realize that she didn't want to get married because in doing so, she would lose who she was as an individual. As she dated each potential mate, she would take on his likes, dislikes, hobbies, and even what he liked to eat.

In one scene, a friend of Maggie's asked her how she liked her eggs cooked. It was a profound moment, because she really didn't know how she liked them. In an unforgettable moment toward the end of the film, Maggie cooked herself eggs in a variety of ways to see which ones *she* liked the best.

How you like your eggs may not be the biggest challenge in your marriage, but maintaining your personal space, preferences, and identity just might be. It's possible that you may not even realize it. When so much of life converges with another human being, it's easy to

When two strong and sure people come together under the Lord, utilizing their gifts, minds, and spirits according to His plan, a greater kingdom impact will occur.

lose who you are and to let your own candle blow out. But the greatest gift you can give your unity is to maintain your individual uniqueness. Because when two strong and sure people come together under the Lord, utilizing their gifts, minds, and spirits according to His plan, a greater kingdom impact will occur.

The Work of the Spirit

Never let unity morph into sameness. Preserve your identities while guarding against division. There's an illustration I love to use about mayonnaise. One of the challenges of making mayonnaise is getting the oil and vinegar to come together. Oil and liquids do not mix, but they are necessary ingredients in mayonnaise. So what the makers of mayonnaise do is introduce an emulsifier into the ingredients.

An emulsifier helps ingredients that are at odds with each other to get along, to blend. So a necessary ingredient in mayonnaise is the emulsifier: eggs. The eggs say, "I want you, oil, over here to hang out with me, and I want you, vinegar, to hang out with me too." When eggs get mixed in with the vinegar and oil, the vinegar and oil will now hang out with each other. Not because vinegar and oil like each other but because both of them can agree on eggs, and as a result, something greater than the individual parts is created—mayonnaise.

The Holy Spirit is the emulsifier in any marriage. When there is ongoing conflict between Christian husbands and wives, one or both parties have ignored the emulsifying work of the Holy Spirit. As a result, they can no longer point to the shared work of the Spirit in their lives, in spite of any differences of taste or opinion that might exist.

Paul emphasized this truth by telling the Ephesian Christians that the relational oneness that characterizes unity is "preserved," not created. They are to "preserve the unity of the Spirit in the bond of peace" (Ephesians 4:3). When it comes to marriage, God is not inviting us to create anything. He's inviting us to preserve what He's already created. We have entered into a relationship with Him through His Spirit, and as a result, He is already present and at work in the midst of our marriages.

Paul's challenge to "preserve the unity of the Spirit" is complemented by his notice that this unity of the Spirit exists "in the bond of peace" (4:3). Paul's concept of peace here is much broader than our modern definition of an absence of conflict or a feeling of harmony. Paul was likely pointing to the Hebrew concept of *shalom*, defined as "wholeness, health, and well-being." Shalom is more than just peace between two parties; it indicates the overall health and balance of an organism. So when we preserve the unity of the Spirit, the outcome is a healthy, balanced marriage in which to fully live out and experience abundant life.

> ✤✤✤✤✤
>
> *A healthy marriage is a unified marriage where the presence and work of God's Spirit transcends our individual differences.*
>
> ✤✤✤✤✤

A healthy marriage is a unified marriage where the presence and work of God's Spirit transcends our individual differences. Satan seeks to disrupt the unity in our marriages in order to bring about disorder, which ultimately leads to chaos.

To combat that, let's transition to looking at how we can use this gauge of the spirit of unity to read our ministry context and move it toward healthy bonds of shalom, or peace.

Reading the Gauge

The primary work for us to do to achieve unity in our marriages is the work of preservation, or perhaps in more modern terminology, the work of conservation. The work of conservation is concerned with protecting the environment from threats that would erode the natural habitat. To do this work well, we need to activate our spiritual monitoring system to give us a good read on our marriage atmosphere. How do we read this gauge of the unity of the Spirit?

In Ephesians 4:2, Paul listed the primary indicators of this unity: humility, gentleness, patience, and tolerance in love. If you want to see how well you are cultivating a spirit of unity in your marriage, take a look at how these four virtues are functioning in your marital relationship. Here are some key diagnostic questions to ask:

1. Humility
   - *Are you willing in the interest of unity to submit your desires, no matter how good, to God's purpose in your marriage?*
   - *Are you willing to serve your mate, looking out for his or her interests above your own (see Philippians 2:3–4)?*

2. Gentleness
   - *Are you argumentative with your mate?*
   - *Do you find yourself responding with anger when your agenda is challenged?*
   - *What is your first, unfiltered response when your mate wrongs you?*

3. Patience
   - *Are you willing to wait on God's work through His Spirit in the life of your mate?*
   - *Do you find yourself impatient with the slowness of change in your mate's life?*
   - *Can you wait on the Spirit and the discernment of your marriage partner before making a change or starting a new interest?*

4. Tolerance in love
    - *Do you insist on things being done your way?*
    - *Can you allow for the diversity of ways and means that the Spirit works through other people?*
    - *Do you work well when your mate's preferences conflict with your own?*

I'd like to propose to you that each of these indicators point toward one primary threat to unity. (There are, of course, other threats to the unity of a marriage, but many of them can be traced back to this primary one.) The presence of this threat should sound the alarm that the unity of the Spirit is under attack, and as a result, your marriage monitoring system should activate some unity preservation/conservation practices that will counteract the threat.

What is this foundational threat to the unity of the Spirit? It is the tendency to elevate our personal agendas over the Spirit's agenda in our marriages. Each of the four indicators in the previous list reflects a life that is willing to submit to the reality of God's work through His Spirit. Do we as individuals and as couples working together possess the humility, gentleness, patience, and love to submit our wills and agendas to God's agenda?

As I noted earlier, Paul was making an important point when he tied unity to the presence of the Spirit in our marriages. The implication here is that if you are not spiritual, or if you have no orientation to the Spirit, then you are going to have a problem preserving unity in your marriage. That's because your point of reference will be the flesh, not the Spirit of God. The flesh is your human understanding, whereas the Spirit represents God's point of view. The conflict that exists in our marriages and threatens unity is really a battle between the flesh and

> *What is this foundational threat to the unity of the Spirit? It is the tendency to elevate our personal agendas over the Spirit's agenda in our marriages.*

the Spirit. That's why Galatians 5:16 tells us, "Walk by the Spirit, and you will not carry out the desire of the flesh." In other words, when our marriages lack unity, it's because the Spirit's control is not being preserved. The Spirit's perspective has been removed, which leads to division, disharmony, and chaos.

Let me say that again: Unresolved, ongoing conflict means the Spirit of God has not been allowed to override the human, fleshly differences that brought about the chaos and are now sustaining that conflict. God has been left out of the equation. We are told to preserve the unity of the Spirit because, if allowed to, the Spirit of God will overrule the human things that bring about and sustain the conflicts we experience in marriage.

James 4:1–2 puts it this way:

What is the source of quarrels and conflicts among you? Is not the source your pleasures that wage war in your members? You lust and do not have; so you commit murder. You are envious and cannot obtain; so you fight and quarrel.

Fighting, conflict, envy, and murder, as James described it, are only symptoms of the deeper, cancerous problem of human, fleshly counteragendas that we often allow to spread and ultimately usurp God's agenda and His presence in our marriages.

Do you know what cancer is? It can be described as cells in the human body that no longer want to be unified and are creating their independent vision and their own program. These radical cells multiply because the agenda of cancerous cells is to take over the entire body. This is often the case in our marriages. A fleshly counteragenda, if unchecked, will spread and usurp "the unity of the Spirit in the bond of peace."

Recalibrating the Gauge

What do we do when the gauges in our spiritual monitoring systems indicate that the unity of the Spirit is at risk in our marriages? The challenge of preserving the unity of the Spirit is that we are fallen, broken people living in a fallen, broken world where we are married to fallen, broken people. To recalibrate our unity gauges, we need to adopt three practices that will promote and preserve a spirit of unity: storytelling, discernment, and peacemaking.

1. *Storytelling.* One of the key things you can do to encourage unity in your marriage is to point out and celebrate the story of God's work through His Spirit in both of your lives. This can best be accomplished by establishing times, as well as an environment, for open communication to flourish. When you begin to do this and see God's work in each of your lives, the source of your unity becomes clear: You are brought together because the Holy Spirit is at work in your lives transforming your sin-scarred hearts into the image of Christ Jesus. You also become more empathetic to the challenges and struggles that each of you face as you hear about each other's struggles.

> *The challenge of preserving the unity of the Spirit is that we are fallen, broken people living in a fallen, broken world where we are married to fallen, broken people.*

2. *Discernment.* The practice of spiritual discernment within your marriage is a critical skill for preserving unity in the bond of peace. Spiritual discernment is decision making that is guided by the Holy Spirit. It is a consensual practice that is oriented toward waiting on the Spirit's voice as the deciding vote in every decision.

A key example of this practice appears in Acts 15 at the Council of Jerusalem. On display here is the practice of Spirit-led discernment at a critical decision point on the issue of Jewish-Gentile relations (the same issue on display in Ephesians). The church heard the witness of key leaders, considered the testimony of Scripture, and waited on the leading of the Spirit until they reached a decision that "seemed good to the Holy Spirit and to us" (15:28).

When marriage partners practice discernment by understanding the voice of the Spirit, filtered through God's Word and applied through godly counsel, decisions can be made that preserve unity. When decisions are made without discernment based on individual preferences, pride, and selfishness, the result will be a spirit of disunity.

3. *Peacemaking.* When they first marry, couples often go through a honeymoon phase when conflict is low, and both partners are discovering the roles they will play in their marriage. It doesn't take long, however, for conflict and

disappointed expectations to appear. Conflict is a part of every relationship that exists in this fallen world, and each of us contributes our sinful, broken self to that conflict. The preservation of unity in our marriages will require the ability to be peacemakers (Matthew 5:9) with the conviction of seeking the rule of God's kingdom in every conflict.

To be peacemakers, we must understand peacemaking and, empowered by the Spirit, apply these practices in our marriages. The best resource I know to assist us in this is Ken Sande's work *The Peacemaker*, in which he details four basic peacemaking practices:

a. Glorify God (1 Corinthians 10:31)—seeking as my first priority to please and honor God in the midst of conflict.

b. Get the log out of your eye (Matthew 7:5)—taking responsibility for our own contribution to the conflict.

c. Gently restore (Galatians 6:1)—serving the other party or parties in love to help them take responsibility for their part in the conflict.

d. Go and be reconciled (Matthew 5:24)—demonstrating God's forgiveness and reconciliation by finding a reasonable solution to conflict.[2]

When I opened this chapter, I noted that the unity of the early American colonies played an important role in helping them defeat their common enemy, Great Britain. They rallied around the motto *E pluribus unum*, "out of the many, one," in spite of their many differences. Once the war was over and Great Britain was defeated, the objective of the colonies shifted to maintaining and preserving the unity that had already been forged during the Revolutionary War. Out of this effort emerged the Constitution, which laid out a program of government that balanced various competing interests for the shared purpose of giving birth to a new nation, the United States of America, and maintaining its unity. The Constitution begins with those famous lines, "We the People of the United States, in Order to form a more perfect Union . . . do ordain and establish this Constitution for the United States of America."

Our marriages are formed under an even more perfect union, "the unity of the Spirit in the bond of peace." It is our mission and calling to monitor and preserve this unity as a witness to the world around us. This is, as you may remember, the final blessing Jesus prayed over His disciples and those who would follow after them, including us, who model Him in marriage: "May [they] all be one; even as You, Father, are in Me and I in You, that they also may be in Us, so that the world may believe that You sent Me" (John 17:21).

The success of your mission to glorify God and make Him known is tied to the unity in your marriage.

This means that the success of your mission to glorify God and make Him known is tied to the unity in your marriage. Do you want the world to look at your marriage as a help or a hindrance to encountering and believing in the Christ who loves us?

PART II

The Function of a
KINGDOM
MARRIAGE

6

❖❖❖❖❖❖

ROLES

WHAT DOES A TYPICAL DAY in your workweek look like? Many of us get up with just enough time to get ready for work, wake up the kids, feed them and pack them off to school, jump in our cars for our long commutes, and arrive at work for a busy day of deadlines and meetings. We then lug ourselves home, quickly have dinner or go out to eat, do some homework with the kids, put them to bed, prepare for the next day, and then fall into bed.

With such busy schedules, fulfilling our roles as husbands or wives can seem like another job tacked on to our regular occupations. However, when we choose to live our lives according to God's Kingdom agenda, one of the first places His priorities should show up is in our marriages.

As we discussed earlier, the family is the fundamental institution in society, so it is crucial that we understand our roles as husbands and wives through God's perspective. Yet in a culture riddled with broken hearts and homes, it is difficult for men and women to find models of godly marriages and families. That's why I want to focus on the roles of husbands and wives in this chapter, using Scripture to explore the practical ways they can fulfill their individual kingdom roles in marriage.

For starters, let's review the definitions of a kingdom man and a kingdom woman. A *kingdom man* is "a male who places himself underneath God's rulership and lives his life submitted to the lordship of Jesus Christ." A *kingdom woman* is "a woman who positions herself under and operates according to the rule of God over every area of her life."

The Role of the Kingdom Husband

I'm going to begin with husbands, since that's where God began in creating Adam, and He ultimately holds the man responsible for the condition of the home. When Adam and Eve disobeyed, God came looking for Adam, not Eve, because he was the one responsible. Husbands, I want to look at four key principles that, when applied, will turn your vow into wow in your marriage.

Loving

A husband's first role is to love his wife. It is easy to be nonchalant about this in a world that uses the word *love* to describe a person's television preferences ("I love football") or favorite foods ("I love fried chicken"). But the kind of love the Bible stipulates that a husband should have for his wife is modeled on Christ's love for His church.

Ephesians 5:25 says the man should love his wife "just as Christ also loved the church and gave Himself up for her." So what does it look like for a husband to model his love for his wife based on Christ's love for His church?

> ❖❖❖❖❖
>
> A kingdom man *is "a male who places himself underneath God's rulership and lives his life submitted to the lordship of Jesus Christ."*
>
> ❖❖❖❖❖

First, Christ gave up His life to deliver His church from sin and death and to save her for a relationship with Him. In other words, the Savior and Deliverer of the church demonstrated a love that was sacrificial and self-giving, looking out for the needs of His bride, the church. Husbands should not be in the marriage first and foremost to get their needs met, but rather they should first look out for the interests and needs of their wives. A husband's love should be characterized by sacrifice for the good of his wife.

In Philippians 2:3–11, Paul dug deeper into this concept of what Christ's sacrificial love looked like. In particular, one trait Paul identified as key is humility, regarding "one another as more important than yourselves" (verse 3). If, as a husband, you find that personal pride or selfishness is a barrier to giving yourself sacrificially for your wife, then you are not loving as Christ loved. True biblical love considers the needs of your mate above your own.

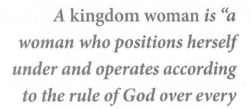

A kingdom woman is "a woman who positions herself under and operates according to the rule of God over every area of her life."

Christ's sacrificial love on behalf of the church was also directed toward a particular purpose. According to Ephesians 5:26–27, Christ loved the church "so that He might sanctify her, having cleansed her by the washing of water with the word, that He might present to Himself the church in all her glory, having no spot or wrinkle or any such thing; but that she would be holy and blameless."

In the Bible, the process of sanctification means to "set apart for special use." It was the process in the Old Testament by which objects were cleaned and purified so that they could be used in the temple. The purpose of Christ's love was to cleanse and purify His bride, the church. The husband should likewise be intimately concerned about the spiritual growth and personal development of his wife.

As a pastor I've seen the opposite of this far too often. In many marriages, the wives, rather than the husbands, are growing spiritually and are concerned for their husbands' growth. A kingdom man will be diligent to take the lead in the area of spiritual intimacy with the Lord so that even if his wife is a close follower of Jesus Christ, he will still have something greater to encourage her toward. Just think how powerful such a marriage union would be!

In addition, Ephesians 5:28–29 says,

So husbands ought also to love their own wives as their own bodies. He who loves his own wife loves himself; for no one ever hated his own flesh, but nourishes and cherishes it, just as Christ also does the church.

Just as the husband "nourishes and cherishes" his own body in order to satisfy its needs, he should also seek to satisfy the needs of his wife. He "nourishes and cherishes" her so that ten, twenty, or thirty years down the line, the wife can say confidently, "I'm satisfied with my life, my purpose, and my marriage."

> *Just as the husband "nourishes and cherishes" his own body in order to satisfy its needs, he should also seek to satisfy the needs of his wife.*

Now most men don't want to hear about crosses and sacrifice. Instead, we want to hear about how we're supposed to be wearing a crown as the king of our castles. Jesus wore an earthly crown before He ever wore the crown in heaven, all right, but it was a crown of thorns. Husband, you won't get the crown of glory without wearing the crown of the cross.

So although most men want to talk about all the good stuff that comes with love, the first thing God wants to know about you as a husband is this: When your wife looks at you, does she see a cross? Are you demonstrating God's love vertically by living with her as a horizontal representation of Jesus?

We men are great at saying the right things. We can sound very impressive to our wives when we want to, talking about how we will be there for them and protect them and even die for them if necessary.

But we're not crazy. We know that the chances of this happening are very remote. I personally can't think of one man I know who has died or even been injured defending his wife from a crazed intruder, and chances are you can't either. That's not going to happen to most of us, or to anyone we know. So we're pretty safe declaring that we would make the ultimate sacrifice for our wives.

But for most of us, it's another story when it comes to the everyday sacrifices of married life—surrendering or yielding our desires, opinions, preferences, and plans for our wives. When God calls husbands to give themselves up for their wives, He is not simply talking about being willing to die. Sacrificing for our wives and loving them involves being willing to nail our desires and agendas to the cross to meet their needs.

This brings us to the area where we fail so often as husbands: selfishness. It's difficult for most men to give up our wants for our wives. Yet a husband should let his love be visible and tangible so that his wife can experience how much he values her.

Anyone who knows me knows I'm a man's man. I love being a man. Everything about me thrills at the idea and reality of manhood. (Just read *Kingdom Man!*) But without fail, when my wife hands me her "bag" to hold for her while she's shopping (I call it a bag, men—that helps), I grab it. Yes, I'm that guy—the one holding her bag. Do I like it? No. Does it make me look manly? No, not according to the world's definition. Do I love my wife? Yes. And this is one small way I visibly demonstrate that love to her.

The question of a husband's sacrifice is very simple: If I gave your wife a piece of paper and asked her to list what you have given up because of what she needs, desires, or cherishes, how long would her list be?

If I asked her to tell me in what ways you have altered your schedule or activities so that she can do something she wants or needs to do, would she have anything to tell me? If the answer is no, then that's the first place you need to start making some changes in your marriage.

I work a lot, and I enjoy it. Not only have I pastored a church for nearly forty years now, but we also have a national ministry, and I speak frequently. Yet I always make room in my week for my wife, men, and so should you. One day each week is dedicated to her. I put my phone away (for the most part), I tackle my honey-do list, we enjoy eating together, talking, and shopping—whatever the case may be. Too many men these days sacrifice their relationship with their wives because of their careers or hobbies, but that is not fulfilling their role in marriage.

Too many men these days sacrifice their relationship with their wives for their careers or hobbies, but that is not fulfilling their role in marriage.

I encourage you to start by seeking to intentionally understand your wife and what she needs from you but is not receiving. Then try to meet as many of those needs as reasonably possible. If you have walled off communication in your marriage to such an extent that you don't even know what your wife wants or needs, and she's too timid to say anything, you need to go to her right now and ask her. You just might be surprised by what she says. But you won't know unless you ask. You may be working on an area you think will satisfy your wife but are missing the mark altogether.

A good friend of mine recently asked his wife what one thing he could do to improve their relationship. He assumed she would say something like "spend more time with the children" or "grow more spiritually." Do you know what she said? "Stop biting your nails."

My friend laughed as he told me that he's had a habit of biting his nails their entire marriage. Apparently this really annoyed her, but she rarely said anything. Knowing this is what his wife wanted most from him gave him not only the ability but also the desire to put that bad habit to rest. So go ahead and ask. It'll take the guesswork out of the mystery of loving well.

The point is that our love should be visible as well as verbal.

Knowing, Honoring, and Praying with Your Wife

The other three roles husbands are to fulfill in marriage are knowing their wives, honoring them, and praying with them. To live with your wife means to dwell in close harmony with her, making your home a place of intimacy and mutual support. Many husbands approach their family life with the attitude that the home and the responsibilities that go with it are primarily the wife's job. However, if the husband is to live with his wife "in an understanding way" (1 Peter 3:7), he must see the home as a primary place to exercise Christ's mandate of sacrificial, self-giving love. The husband must be committed to the home as a place of vocation and calling in addition to his workplace. Whenever the things you do for your wife outside of your home (such as your career) diminish your presence with her to a large degree, then you are not living with her in the way 1 Peter 3:7 describes.

To live with your wife "in an understanding way" also means that the husband is responsible for intimately knowing his wife. This means that he must be committed to taking the time to come to know her and making necessary adjustments in his schedule to open up space for that.

Another role of the husband is to "honor" his wife "as a fellow heir of the grace of life" (verse 7). To grant honor to your wife is to place her in a position of significance and treat her as someone unique. Whether through kind words, special gifts, or notes telling her how much you love her, you have a responsibility to let your wife know that she is special.

A true commitment to honor your wife means more than just honoring her on special days (birthdays, anniversaries, Valentine's Day); it means consistently communicating to her the value you place on your relationship. Just as God's lovingkindnesses are new every morning (Lamentations 3:22–23), so we as kingdom leaders should show that same consistency to our wives.

The husband's mandate to honor his wife is rooted in the recognition that she is "a fellow heir of the grace of life." Though the wife is called to submit to her husband, this is a relationship of function, not a statement of her inequality as a person. Like the man, she's created in the image of God and worthy of honor as the man's spiritual equal in the eyes of God. Do you treat and view your wife as an equal? One way to know if you do is whether you seek her counsel when you are faced with a decision. Another way is if you seek her company when you have free time or leisure time.

Finally, a husband's role is to pray with his wife. At the root of the command for the husband to live with his wife in an understanding way (to know her) and honor her is this warning: "so that your prayers will not be hindered" (1 Peter 3:7). Since the wife is a "fellow heir of the grace of life," God will not do anything for the husband unless the wife is included. God views the marriage covenant as entering into a "one flesh" relationship; thus, the wife is now included in any interaction God has

> *Since the wife is a "fellow heir of the grace of life," God will not do anything for the husband unless the wife is included.*

with the husband. The husband, then, must be committed to praying with his wife so that together they can reap the spiritual benefits of God's kingdom plan.

Husbands, as leaders, are the spiritual thermostats of their marriages and families, setting the spiritual temperature of the home. The wife, however, is the thermometer, indicating the actual temperature readings in the home. To know whether a man is following God's Kingdom agenda for his home, the best place to look is at his wife. Does she feel loved, known, honored, and spiritually encouraged in her relationship with her husband? If the answer is no, then the husband must inspect his thermostat for damage and reinvest his time and resources into fulfilling his role as a kingdom man and husband. Husbands, if you want a summer wife, then don't bring home winter weather.

The Role of the Kingdom Wife

To borrow a phrase from a popular book, ladies, I'd like you to "lean in" on this part. Because far too often, religion, culture, and the like have sorely diminished the role of the woman—to everyone's detriment. You, as a wife, are a critical piece in the puzzle of advancing God's kingdom on earth.

Not too long ago, I was browsing the Internet (yes, I do have an iPad!) and came across a cover story in *Christianity Today* titled "50 Women You Should Know." Granted, my eyes were drawn to the article because my daughter Priscilla is mentioned in it as one of the fifty women, and she's a force to be reckoned with for God's kingdom. But what caught my attention as I began to read was the subhead of the article, which said, "We asked key leaders which Christian women are most profoundly shaping the evangelical church and North American society. This is who they picked."[1]

That statement grabbed me, in particular, because while all fifty of these women have certainly had a profound impact on the church and our culture through their various ministries or political influence, there are countless unknown women who may have had or are having an even greater influence. These women do it through the children they raise who grow up and become spiritual influencers, leaders, marketplace front-runners, writers, singers, and the like. These women also do it through the men they support as wives.

Behind every kingdom man is a kingdom woman, and I guarantee you that the influential men who would be on any list of "50 Men You Should Know" today might not be there at all without their wives, who believed in them from the start, sacrificed for them as they grew, loved them through their learning, and strategized with them during those late-night hours or early morning conversations over coffee.

The powerful force of a kingdom wife cannot be overstated.

Many men have gone on to do great things, bigger and larger than they ever aspired to, simply because they had wives who believed in them and urged them on. They had wives who steered them away from that which was only a distraction and toward that which was most profitable for God and His kingdom. They had wives who spent time in the silence of an inner room praying for their husbands when it didn't seem as though they were on track to make much of a difference at all.

I agree with applauding women of influence as *Christianity Today* did, but I don't think they thoroughly captured or reflected all of the women of greatest influence in our nation today. So, ladies, lean in, because what I have to say right now may be very different from what you've heard about the role of a wife. When God created Eve for Adam (the woman to connect with the man), He did so for a specific purpose, and that purpose is much more significant than most of us ever realize.

> *Many men have gone on to do great things, bigger and larger than they ever aspired to, simply because they had wives who believed in them and urged them on.*

Much of the confusion we experience in our marriages today comes from an inaccurate view of this purpose. When we read that God said it wasn't good for Adam to be alone, we assume that Eve came along to provide companionship. But if God had created Eve for companionship, then Adam probably would have said that he didn't like being alone. But it was God who said that, not Adam. That's an important point we often skip over, so let that sink in. Also, the Hebrew words used to describe the woman as a "helper" don't refer to someone who relieves loneliness. It refers to someone who provides viable and visible help.

There is only one reason God would say, "I will make him a helper suitable for him" (Genesis 2:18), and it's that Adam obviously needed help.

I'm not negating the importance of companionship, friendship, and relationship in marriage. But based on the historical law of first mention with regard to marriage in the Bible, companionship for Adam wasn't God's primary concern when He made the woman. It was about empowering Adam to exercise rule in God's name at an even greater level than he could alone.

The Hebrew words translated "helper suitable for him" in Genesis 2:18 are surprisingly powerful terms. They are *ezer*[2] and *kenegdo*.[3] *Ezer* appears twenty-one times in the Old Testament, only two of which refer to a woman. The other instances refer to God Himself providing help at a superior level (e.g., Deuteronomy 33:26; Psalms 33:20; 70:5; 124:8).

> *As a wife, you have a high calling to discover with your spouse how God wants the two of you to best use your skills, talents, time, and treasure to advance His kingdom on this earth.*

To set *ezer* apart from every other use in the Old Testament referring to a stronger help brought by God, the word *kenegdo* was added. *Kenegdo* literally means "before your face, within your view or purpose."[4] Some have translated it as "a completion of" or "a counterpart to."

Wives, if you view your role as only cooking food, cleaning the house, wiping noses, driving kids to soccer or dance practice, and so on, you have missed your role. Chores are necessary and food is important, but depending on where you are in this stage of your life, you could hire someone for those tasks, or your husband could share the load. As a wife, you have a high calling to discover with your spouse how God wants the two of you to best use your skills, talents, time, and treasure to advance His kingdom on this earth.

Eve was created for much more than being a maid. According to the contextual definition of a "helper suitable for him," she was created to be a "strong help" in the position of a "counterpart." Advancing in your destinies as husband and wife is a collaborative effort if you want to advance well individually and collectively.

My wife, Lois, is very different from me both in temperament and skill sets. But God has greatly used her passion for detail and her administrative gifts to help launch and develop our church and our national ministry. She has been and continues to be an essential collaborator for the kingdom purpose of our marriage, and that purpose transcends personal happiness.

An often-overlooked Scripture that supports this is found in Proverbs: "Her husband is known in the gates, when he sits among the elders of the land" (31:23). The "gates" in biblical times signified that place where the leaders of the township would gather to discuss important news and happenings. This woman's husband didn't get there on his own. The very fact that he rose to such great influence in his city backs up what I said earlier that many women will never make *Christianity Today*'s "50 Women You Should Know" list but should. If this is you, my friend, don't despair. God has His own list, and His rewards last a lot longer than temporal applause and attention on this earth.

Any man who doesn't view his wife as a strong help and counterpart or look to her for her skills, insight, intellect, training, and giftedness is a foolish man. Any man who doesn't actively encourage his wife and provide a way for her to sharpen her skills, intellect, and training is an equally foolish man. To undervalue your wife and her role, husbands, is one of the gravest mistakes you could ever make.

Unfortunately, some traditional teaching on the roles of men and women in the home have painted a picture that doesn't reflect *ezer kenegdo* accurately. Cultural norms and teachings have distorted the views of many women and men regarding how essential the woman's role is, and this distortion has been one of the major contributors to the lack of advancement of God's kingdom on earth. This isn't to say that a woman's only purpose is to help her husband, as we clearly see in the example of the Proverbs 31 wife. But regarding the nature of the relationship between husband and wife, her help to him is a lot different from what most of us have envisioned it to be.

Uh-Oh, the S-Word

You didn't think I'd write a chapter on roles in marriage without going here, did you? Submission is worse than a four-letter word in our society today. I get that. I hear it in counseling. I've seen the demise of far too many marriages because that word has been misused. Most women would rather die than live their lives locked in the minivan, chained to the stove, or amicably acquiescing to all of their husbands' decisions (a common misconception of submission). That's not the biblical picture of submission at all. Submission refers to a hierarchical order that should be called upon only when necessary.

> *Submission refers to a hierarchical order that should be called upon only when necessary.*

The greatest illustration of submission came not too long ago when I was invited with my family to attend a special screening of the movie *War Room*, which stars my daughter Priscilla. As you may know, the Kendrick brothers wrote, produced, and directed this movie. These two men have done an excellent job of setting biblical principles into story form so that we can all benefit and be discipled through the arts.

After the movie was over, the Kendrick brothers wanted our feedback, so we had a time for reflection and questions. But I had a question for them. "Who gets to have the final say," I asked, "if you disagree on a certain take or dialogue in the movie. Who decides?"

Both of the brothers smiled, and then one replied, "It depends on who owns it," he said. "We rarely disagree to the point that one of us has to trump the other, but depending on what project it is—or what part of a project—we've assigned which one of us is the lead. And whoever is the lead has the final say."

They both laughed and made some jokes, and then we moved on to talk more about the movie. I could tell by their utter joy in discussing what they do that the issue of "submitting" to the "lead," as they called it, was not an issue at all. Each trusted the other's judgment and position.

What a wonderful picture of marriage. As the brothers said, rarely did it ever get to the point where one person had to have the final say. They operated and moved in such great unison toward the same vision and goal that they were most often able to come to an agreement of sorts. But if push ever came to shove, someone made a decision, and the other followed. The other "submitted."

Jesus is the best example of submission lived out in the flesh. Most of the time, He and God were on the same page. But when they weren't, and He asked God to take the cup of suffering and death from Him, He ultimately submitted to His Father's will (Matthew 26:36–46). Jesus *chose* to place Himself under God the Father's authority even though they were both equal and had all the characteristics of divinity.

The key word in Jesus's divine example of submission is *choice*. It wasn't force. Submission that must be forced is not submission. Nor is the submission of the wife to her husband absolute, since her greater commitment is to the Lord.

So why is submission such a misunderstood and misapplied marriage principle? Many women feel unappreciated and unrecognized for their contributions to the home—for their *ezer kenegdo*. When we get that wrong, a whole lot becomes wrong after it. Because of this, submission can seem like surrender—surrender to the status quo, surrender to a lack of recognition or value, or even surrender to boredom and a lack of purpose, meaning, and passion for life.

When a woman truly learns how to submit and does so biblically as to the Lord, this opens the door for God to operate on her behalf in the life of her husband.

But just the opposite is true! When a woman truly learns how to submit and does so biblically as to the Lord, this opens the door for God to operate on her behalf in the life of her husband.

Submission comes from the Greek word *hupotasso*, which means "to willingly place oneself under the authority of another." This is what Christ demonstrated on the cross. We looked at this in more detail in the chapter on order, but it bears repeating here that God calls husbands to willingly place themselves under Christ (1 Corinthians 11:3) and wives to willingly place themselves under God and their husbands. Again, submission doesn't indicate an inferior status or value. When God calls wives to submit to their husbands, He asks them to trust in His design for marriage.

Satan's Great Reversal

When Satan tempted Eve in the garden of Eden, he wanted to turn the order in marriage on its head. Satan is happy when wives assume the leadership role over their husbands. But just as God held Adam responsible for failing to lead Eve well in the garden, He will hold men accountable for abdicating their role in the family. And just as Eve was at fault for ignoring Adam's leadership as he stood with her in the presence of the Serpent, God will hold wives accountable for disregarding their husbands' legitimate headship.

> *When a wife is willing to surrender herself first to the Lord, only then will she be able to properly submit to her husband.*

After Adam and Eve fell to Satan's temptation, a curse fell on all of creation. God told Eve that as a result of her disobedience, she and all of her female descendants would want to take leadership in the family, but their husbands would desire to dominate them (Genesis 3:16). Thankfully, Christ has reversed the curse and gives wives and husbands the grace to live in harmony according to God's original design.

It's pretty easy for a wife to submit to her husband if he loves the Lord and walks in obedience to Him. But what if he doesn't? Does God still require submission if a husband isn't living as a Christian? Here's a better question: Can God still lead a family when the husband isn't walking with Him? Yes. God is sovereign, and wives can surrender completely to Him, trusting that He will not only work through a disobedient husband, but He can transform that husband's heart through the honor and respect his wife shows him.

When a wife is willing to surrender herself *first* to the Lord, only then will she be able to properly submit to her husband. And when God sees that a wife trusts in Him enough to honor her husband's role, He will work in amazing and even miraculous ways to bless and guide her family, just as He did for Sarah (1 Peter 3:6).

7

✤✤✤✤✤✤

RESOLUTIONS

A HUSBAND ONCE SHARED with a friend his secret to making his marriage last. "We go to a nice restaurant once a week and enjoy a good meal and some relaxing music."

To which his friend replied, "Wow! That does sound nice."

"It is," the husband responded. "She goes on Tuesdays, and I go on Fridays."

Another man shared that the secret to his marriage is that he and his wife agreed to never go to bed angry at each other. It sounded like a good plan; however, as a result, they haven't slept together in years.

Although the marriage relationship is one of the most rewarding relationships we can enjoy, it can also be one of the most challenging. No other relationship requires such an intense and ongoing level of mutual exchange and sharing of resources, emotions, communication, patience, passion, and more. Simply by its design, the marriage partnership sets itself up to be one of the most testing, trying, or even exhausting engagements in life. It's no wonder so many couples end up divorced, and so many who do stay married do so out of obligation rather than desire or love.

> *Although the marriage relationship is one of the most rewarding relationships we can enjoy, it can also be one of the most challenging.*

What I want to encourage you to consider in this chapter, though, is the value of the sanctifying effect of marriage. As Gary Thomas writes, "What if God designed marriage to make us holy more than to make us happy?"[1] When we make seeking and serving God our highest calling, as it should be, then anything that equips or enables us to do this better ought to be embraced.

God will often use the things and people closest to us to do the greatest work in our hearts, minds, and souls. What we need to remember in these situations of conflict is that God always has a purpose for the pain (Romans 8:28) when we commit that pain to Him and His will. Your spouse is not your enemy but rather is a tool God sometimes allows to soften your edges, strengthen your weak spots, and deepen the authenticity of both your faith and your love.

A man I had been counseling came up to me at church one day after the service and said, "Pastor, my wife is killing me."

I smiled, put my hand on his shoulder, and said, "You did tell me you wanted to be more like Jesus, didn't you?"

In all of our lives, we must die to our selves (our flesh or sinful nature) in order for the fullness of God's Holy Spirit to dwell within us and manifest His fruit. Unfortunately for most marriages, this union can provide some of the greatest opportunities for this death to occur.

> *God will often use the things and people closest to us to do the greatest work in our hearts, minds, and souls.*

Now, if you are one of the few husbands or wives who have a rosy extended honeymoon, then maybe this chapter isn't for you. But after decades of counseling couples whose marriages appeared to be rosy on the outside but weren't under the surface, I have a hunch that this chapter applies to more of us than we would like to admit. With marriage comes conflict—whether it's competing values, preferences, desires, traits, or even control. Whatever causes conflict in your marriage, if you and your spouse will learn how to view it through the lens of God's love, you can grow from it rather than allow it to destroy you.

The Purpose of the Thorn

One of the best passages on having a kingdom-based view of hardship or conflict is found in the apostle Paul's second letter to the church at Corinth. It's a familiar passage to most who attend church regularly, but rarely is it applied directly to marriage. It reads,

> Because of the surpassing greatness of the revelations, for this reason, to keep me from exalting myself, there was given me a thorn in the flesh, a messenger of Satan to torment me—to keep me from exalting myself! (2 Corinthians 12:7)

Before we dig deeper, I want to caution you not to view your spouse as "a messenger of Satan" or a "thorn in the flesh." Your spouse is a gift God has given you to better enable you to carry out your divine destiny in life. We need to be careful to make that distinction before diving into this passage. However, God can and often does use people—even the Devil—to develop our spiritual maturity and character.

The Greek word for "thorn" in this passage refers to something that causes irritation. It's like a splinter shaved off a piece of wood that gets caught under your skin. It involves anything that causes ongoing exasperation, frustration, or irritation. But remember, the person is not the thorn; he or she is simply the vehicle through which God allows the thorn to come.

The thorn could refer to that thing your spouse does, or does not do, that always invokes your sigh. Or a difference in perspective that the two of you have never been able to resolve. It could be any number of things. The Bible never tells us what Paul's specific "thorn" was that the

> ❖❖❖❖❖
>
> *The thorn is something God gives or allows that causes pain or weariness for an intended spiritual purpose.*
>
> ❖❖❖❖❖

Lord caused him to experience. Some say it was poor eyesight, while others speculate that it may have been loneliness. But since the term *messenger* is used, it is highly possible that the thorn was a person being used by the Devil to irritate him. Whatever the case, the principle remains the same: A thorn is something God gives or allows that causes pain or weariness for an intended spiritual purpose.

Some of us deal with emotional thorns in our marriages. These are things that have to do with our feelings. It could be loneliness. In fact, some of the loneliest people I know are married couples. This is because the relationship lacks authentic connection or friendship, which leaves the couple feeling isolated. They may be together, but they feel alone. Some other emotional thorns could be depression, regret, pain, and a common thorn in marriages: bitterness.

Some couples deal more with relational thorns. This is when the personalities, quirks, bents, or preferences of their mates simply annoy them. While there are no biblical grounds for divorce, neither is any attraction, affection, or appreciation evident in the marriages. These couples often feel stuck spiritually, unhappy because their needs are not being met but also feeling unable to do anything substantial to change that reality.

I've seen marriages battered down by financial thorns as well. Despite two incomes, couples find it difficult to make ends meet. Rarely do they experience the freedom to enjoy the fruits of their labor. Or perhaps due to financial difficulties, they are stuck in unhappy work situations that then overflow into their marital relationships and homes. And just when it looks as though they might be climbing out the pit of debt, some other expense arises that keeps them there. They just can't seem to shake the financial storms.

And then there are the physical thorns. These are health issues, such as chronic illnesses, headaches that won't go away, disabilities, low energy, cancer, or any number of other ailments. Marriages do not look promising when plagued by health issues. Statistics say that over 75 percent of struggling marriages end in divorce when one partner has a chronic illness.[2] Those aren't very good odds at all. The stress of health-related problems frequently takes its toll on couples. One gentleman, who had nursed his wife with multiple sclerosis for more than two decades, told me that they used to attend MS conferences once a year, but they stopped going because they were saddened to see so many spouses whose mates had abandoned them when they came down with the chronic disease. They said they rarely saw married couples attend; most of the partners had left.

Thorns come in all shapes and sizes, yet regardless of their magnitude or sharpness, a thorn always hurts. If you've ever walked in a Texas yard barefoot, you know what I mean. You can barely see the tiny barbs on the end of the thistles growing in the grass, but they hurt bad enough to stop you right in your tracks.

No one likes a thorn, no matter how big or small. So the first principle to start applying in our marriages is to admit that *marriage comes with thorns simply because both husbands and wives are human.* Marriage comes with pain. To ignore that reality, or to dismiss it, will only make the wounds fester and grow rather than accomplish what they were designed to do, which is to mature us into the likeness of Jesus Christ.

The second principle to apply in our marriages is to recognize that *thorns are a gift.* The apostle Paul claimed, "There was *given* me a thorn in the flesh" (2 Corinthians 12:7). Paul didn't stumble upon this thorn. He didn't happen upon it while out walking one day. He didn't bump into it, nor did it chase him down. This thorn, which brought him pain, was "given" to him by God through a "messenger of Satan."

Apparently God is in the thorn-giving business after all. That's not something we hear much about in these days of the cosmic Santa Claus God who is supposed to bless us, prosper us, and expand our borders with His favor. Though God does do those things, we must not forget that

> *Marriage comes with pain. To ignore that reality, or to dismiss it, will only make the wounds fester and grow.*

He is also very interested in developing us along the way. One of the worst things that could ever happen to a person would be to arrive at his or her destiny and yet still be too spiritually immature to live it out fully. The opportunity then gets wasted or not maximized.

This is why one of the most dangerous prayers you can pray for your marriage is for God to bless you. The road to blessing is often littered with lessons to be learned first and faith to be developed. These lessons strengthen your character, cultivate your virtues, and deepen your love so that when you receive God's blessings, you won't squander them because of your own uselessness as a believer. I know that *uselessness* may sound like a harsh word, but it's not my word; it's the apostle Peter's. So take it up with him when you see him! Peter reminds us of the many layers of our personal development that we must embrace and live out so that we won't live "useless" lives:

> Now for this very reason also, applying all diligence, in your faith supply moral excellence, and in your moral excellence, knowledge, and in your knowledge, self-control, and in your self-control, perseverance, and in your perseverance, godliness, and in your godliness, brotherly kindness, and in your brotherly kindness, love. For if these qualities are yours and are increasing, they render you neither useless nor unfruitful in the true knowledge of our Lord Jesus Christ. (2 Peter 1:5–8)

When you pray that God will help you love your spouse more completely, or that your spouse will love you more deeply, remember the path that teaches and cultivates love. It includes self-control, perseverance, kindness, and more.

When you pray that God will help you love your spouse more completely, or that your spouse will love you more deeply, remember the path that teaches and cultivates love.

Last I checked, virtues like that don't just sprout on their own. Rather, they are developed over time and often through trial by way of thorns.

Learning from the Thorn

How do you know when you are facing a thorn? Because it won't go away. In 2 Corinthians 12:8 we read, "Concerning this I implored the Lord three times that it might leave me." Paul's thorn was needling him, and it wouldn't quit, despite his time in prayer with the Lord. When that is the case in your marriage, consider instead what God may be wanting to accomplish through the issue you are facing. Far too many of us are simply trying to get rid of something that God Himself gave us. God gave Paul his thorn by way of Satan, because God had something He wanted to develop in Paul: He wanted Paul to learn to rely on Him for his strength.

If you have been praying about something in your relationship, and it doesn't seem like God has been addressing your prayer, removing the issue, or providing a solution, go to Him the next time you pray and ask Him what He wants to teach you and your spouse through this thorn.

One of the reasons God gives you a thorn is because He wants to show you something new. He wants you to see something beyond your normal comprehension, and He wouldn't easily get your attention without it.

Far too many believers are satisfied with living normal lives rather than the abundant life Christ died to provide. Because of this, they spend their time complaining about their thorns and trying to cover up the pain with distractions rather than asking the Lord what He wants to teach them that will take them to their next level of spiritual maturity.

The athletes on professional athletic teams didn't get there without a significant amount of pain. To develop their muscles and fine-tune their skills, they had to exercise, practice, and prepare themselves. They had to intentionally experience thorns to get them where they needed to be. Similarly, no mature believer gets there merely by wishing to be there. Growth comes through discipline, learning, and applying God's truths to life's scenarios. Maturity in your marriage will be achieved as you both seek God's wisdom about the thorns He allows you to experience rather than resenting each other for being the one delivering the lesson.

Another reason God gives thorns in our marriages is to keep us from exalting ourselves. Paul said, "To keep me from exalting myself, there was given me a thorn in the flesh" (2 Corinthians 12:7). Thorns remind us that we are human, like everyone else. They keep us dependent on God. Our tendency, without thorns, is to forget our need for God. How different is your prayer life and time in God's Word when you are going through a trial versus when everything seems to be sailing along smoothly? Trials and thorns drive most of us to our knees. God doesn't want us to forget where the source of all abundant living in our marriages really comes from.

A third reason God allows a thorn in our lives is to address an actual, or even a potential, sin in us. The thorn can be, although it is not always, disciplinary in nature (Hebrews 12:8–11). Sometimes when God allows circumstances, people, or situations to stick us, it's because He wants to address something we may not have seen or been willing to repent of without the thorn. At a bare minimum, He wants to address the sin of our pride and self-sufficiency.

Your Response to the Thorn

As we saw earlier, the apostle Paul responded to his thorn first in prayer. He "implored the Lord" to get rid of it (2 Corinthians 12:8). Following Paul's example, we should also pray first about the thorns we are experiencing in our marriages. For your marriage to reach its greatest potential in both fulfillment and purpose, it needs to be bathed regularly in prayer. Rather than complaining about the thorn that irritates you, take it to the Lord and ask if He will remove it. He might do just that. But if the answer is no, and the Lord has not removed the thorn after multiple requests, then seek God's wisdom about what He wants you to learn in the midst of it. And seek God's strength to bear it well just as God told Paul to do. God didn't remove his thorn, but He gave Paul a bit of insight: "My grace is sufficient for you, for power is perfected in weakness" (verse 9).

Thorns remind us that we are human, like everyone else.

My translation reads like this: "I'm not going to grant your request, Paul, but I will meet your need." In the meantime, while God was meeting Paul's need for grace to handle the thorn he had been dealt, God was also perfecting Paul's power to live the abundant life. He was developing Paul for a purpose yet to come.

God doesn't always answer yes. If He did, His sovereignty would not be possible. And we would be in a world of hurt. When you look back over your life and the things that you have asked for in prayer, how many nos are you now grateful for? They say that hindsight is twenty-twenty, but God always sees with perfect vision—past, present, and future.

While God may not remove the thorn by answering yes to your prayers, I can assure you that if you are enduring a thorn that He refuses to get rid of, He will also supply sufficient grace for you to handle it. This is a promise based on God's Word, found in what I consider to be the greatest verse on grace in the entire Bible: "God is able to make all grace abound to you, so that always having all sufficiency in everything, you may have an abundance for every good deed" (2 Corinthians 9:8). The pool of God's grace is available to you when you need it. You just need to access it by relying on His strength and focusing on His will in the midst of your pain and trials.

When you are dealing with a thorn in your relationship with your spouse and have committed it to prayer, and yet God has not removed it, ask Him for His grace. Don't try to pull that thorn out yourself, because you are going to rip something. Rather, go searching for God's grace. The difference between a defeated marriage and a victorious marriage with the same thorn is that the victorious couple is experiencing grace while the other couple is trying to fix things on their own. One marriage is resting under the spiritual cover of grace, while the other is battling things out in the physical realm.

> *If you are enduring a thorn that He refuses to get rid of, He will also supply sufficient grace for you to handle it.*

There are always two ways of dealing with any problem in your marriage. One way is to get rid of the problem. There's nothing wrong with that. If the problem can be solved effectively, then do it. But the other way is to have something happen in your marriage at such a superior level that it causes you to forget the problem or to no longer view it as a problem, but rather to view it through a spiritual lens of learning. For example, let's say you suffer from depression, but when you go out to the mailbox today or tomorrow, you pull out a legitimate check for a million dollars. Do you think you're going to feel depressed that day? It's doubtful simply because something so devastatingly glorious has trumped the thorn, making it seem less significant.

Married couple, we serve a God who can do exceedingly abundantly above the devastatingly glorious in your home and in your marriage, if you will pull off your gloves, stop viewing each other as the thorn itself, and seek His purpose in it. When you spend your life running from your thorns, you will miss the revelation and illumination—and the grace—God wants to give you.

We've all been to the doctor, and at some point we've all been stuck by a needle that pricks. That needle irritates us and even causes many of us to hate needles, and maybe even doctors. But inside the prick of that needle is medicine that's designed for your benefit and your good. The same thing hurting you is also helping you. Yet if you tell the nurse, "Don't stick me, because that needle hurts," you might be rid of the immediate pain, but you are also rid of the medication and what you have to gain from it—good health.

> *Stop viewing each other as the thorn itself, and seek His purpose in it.*

If God is sticking your marriage and your relationship somehow right now—if there is something that's truly irritating you—then pray and ask Him to fix it or remove it. But if He doesn't, you need to accept that He has medicine in the thorn that will bring you and your marriage into better health.

The apostle Paul learned his lesson about his thorn. We know this by his response. If you make his response your own in your marriage, you will be amazed at how strong God makes you. You will be able to handle things that used to cause you to lose your temper. Things you used to say that were disrespectful won't escape your lips. Bitterness, anger, or suspicion that you used to harbor regularly will be replaced with peace and trust.

Paul said,

> Most gladly, therefore, I will rather boast about my weaknesses,
> so that the power of Christ may dwell in me. Therefore I am
> well content with weaknesses, with insults, with distresses, with
> persecutions, with difficulties, for Christ's sake; for when I am weak,
> then I am strong. (2 Corinthians 12:9–10)

Paul not only accepted his thorn; he bragged about it. He praised God for his weaknesses, because in his weaknesses he discovered his true strength. Complaining, whining, or saying, "It's not fair" or "I'm too fine a woman for that insensitive husband" is not bragging about your thorn. Bragging involves approaching God's throne to praise Him for supplying the grace you need to grow in it. It is learning the secret power of contentment and gratitude, knowing that God has allowed the thorn for your good and the good of your relationship.

Oysters and clams get irritated regularly. Whenever sand gets inside their shells, it becomes an irritant. The problem is that the oyster, like Paul, can't get rid of what is pricking it. But what the oyster does instead is secrete a liquid onto the sand. And as the oyster continues to secrete the liquid around the irritant, that grain of sand gets transformed into a pearl. It becomes something valuable and expensive because it was allowed to remain for its intended purpose.

When God's grace covers that thorn, it will become a blessing at some level if you stop fighting it.

God's grace is all you need to transform the thorns in your marriage into pearls of great value. When His grace covers that thorn, it will become a blessing at some level if you stop fighting it and yield to it, seeking His wisdom and strength.

8

❖❖❖❖❖❖

REQUESTS

ALL OF US HAVE SPARE TIRES in our cars, just in case. We've got the spare stored in the trunk for that time when we experience a slow leak or a flat. Most of the time we don't even think about the spare tire until something goes wrong. Yet when that something does go wrong, we quickly go to the trunk and grab the spare to help us out of a bad situation.

For far too many couples today, prayer is like a spare tire—stored away, just in case. It's too easy to forget about it until you feel you need it to get out of a messed-up situation. And even then, as marriages crumble, prayer is often an overlooked component. Spouses are too angry with their mates to consider praying for them. Or they're like one woman who told me she was disappointed in my counseling. When I asked her why, she said it was because her husband was improving, and now she had no excuse to divorce him. When hearts have become as hard as that, prayer has long lost its value.

Many of our marriages are anemic because our prayer lives are anemic. Many of our relationships are empty because our prayer lives are empty. Many of our sexual encounters with each other are subpar because our prayer lives are subpar. Many of our homes are filled with conflict and chaos because we have failed to access the one vital tool that could establish peace: prayer.

Prayer in our marriages is often akin to the national anthem before a football game. It gets the game started but has no connection with what happens on the field. It's a courtesy we say before meals, or before sleeping, or possibly before heading out on a trip. But that's it. And so prayer is turned to in times of either courtesy or crisis, but it is rarely used on an ongoing basis to access all that God has in store for our lives and our marriages.

I want us to look at prayer together through the eyes of Paul. I've chosen Paul's insight into prayer because of where he was when he penned his letter to the church at Philippi: jail.

Many of our homes are filled with conflict and chaos because we have failed to access the one vital tool that could establish peace: prayer.

Now I know that marriage is not the same as jail, but having counseled more than a thousand couples over the course of many years, I've heard jail used as an analogy far too often. Spouses sometimes feel trapped in a system of compromise that limits their liberty while repressing their voices. They feel that while they have to make changes to please their partners, their partners do very little to please them. I don't believe this is always an accurate feeling, but it's a common one.

So Paul was in jail, a fitting setting to help us discover something about the power of prayer in marriage. We learn in Paul's letter to the Philippians that not only was he in jail; he was also poor, he didn't know whether he would live or be executed, he had enemies working against him inside the prison, and he had to deal with the conflicts of others outside the prison as well. If anyone deserved a pass on prayer, it would have been Paul. If anyone deserved to toss up their hands and say, "Hey, I'm in a hopeless situation. You pray for me, because I'm on empty," it would have been Paul. Yet instead, Paul taught us some of the greatest truths about prayer as he sat in jail, surrounded by turmoil, anxiety, and conflict.

If Paul could not only practice prayer in his situation but could also encourage others to do the same, then you and I have no excuse for not applying the principles of prayer in our marriages. And to those of you whose marriages are already fairly decent—not at crisis level or feeling like a prison to you—the following principles will help you and your mate reach an even deeper level of trust, intimacy, and shared purpose. They are for all of us, but again, they are used far too infrequently.

Worry About Nothing

Paul began his treatise on entreating God with these words, "Be anxious for nothing" (Philippians 4:6). Even if that's all we learn and apply to our marriages, we'd save a lot of heartache. Anxiety is a plague that targets way too many of us these days. More and more people are turning to antianxiety medications than ever before. Anxiety and worry hover at the base of a good amount of marital conflict. Whether it's anxiety over finances, health, meeting relational needs, the future, or even whether a spouse is being honest and faithful, any number of things can produce feelings of anxiety.

Yet Paul, in the midst of prison and under the weight of possible execution, tells us to be anxious for nothing. He didn't say be anxious about almost nothing, or even be anxious about big things but not little things. Paul told us clearly to be anxious for *nothing*.

How does this relate to your prayer life? It sets the tone, mind-set, and atmosphere that you are not only to enter into prayer with but also to keep within you throughout the day. After all, Paul did tell us to "pray without ceasing" (1 Thessalonians 5:17). That doesn't mean you walk around reciting prayers all day, but rather that in all things you do and say, you include the Lord and His perspective accordingly.

God is not a compartmentalized God—He is King, creator, and ruler over all. Because of this, His worldview and perspective ought to come to bear in all we do. Praying without ceasing augments an ongoing abiding with Christ, which we have been instructed to do so that our lives might be abundant and our prayers might be answered. Jesus spoke about the action and benefits of praying "without ceasing" when He said, "If you abide in Me, and My words abide in you, ask whatever you wish, and it will be done for you" (John 15:7).

> *Anxiety and worry hover at the base of a good amount of marital conflict.*

But you can't be worrying and abiding in Christ. Those two things are mutually exclusive, just as you can't be in the water and not be wet. Jesus *is* your peace (Ephesians 2:14). Knowing this, Paul set the framework for fellowship with God in prayer by instructing us not to be anxious. If you have a weak prayer life, you are going to have a high worry life.

Pray About Everything

First Paul tells us to worry about nothing, and then he tells us "but in everything by prayer and supplication with thanksgiving let your requests be made known to God." (Philippians 4:6). Paul used four words for prayer in this verse: prayer, supplication, thanksgiving, and requests. The first word, *prayer*, has to do with general communication with God. The second word, *supplication*, involves an attitude of appealing to God. The third word, *thanksgiving*, expresses our gratitude to God. And the fourth word, *request*, has to do with being very specific about what we are asking Him to do.

———— ✤✤✤✤✤ ————

If you have a weak prayer life, you are going to have a high worry life.

———— ✤✤✤✤✤ ————

When you follow Paul's outline for prayer, it will decrease your propensity to worry. Worry about nothing and pray about everything. If you applied only these two principles from this entire book in your marriage, you would still see drastic improvements. This is because prayer coupled with faith (a lack of worry) is that powerful (Mark 11:23). If faith can move a mountain, it can make your marriage great.

As I mentioned earlier, my daughter Priscilla recently starred in a movie called *War Room*, in which prayer was the plot of the film.[1] In this movie, Priscilla played a character named Elizabeth Jordan, the wife in a marriage that had gone bad. Elizabeth's frustration and anger had contributed to the distance in and the demise of her relationship with her husband, Tony. But as she was struggling, she met a woman who devoted herself to mentoring her in prayer.

This elderly woman told her about doing "battle" in the "war room"—her closet. She taught Elizabeth to take her troubles and her worries about her husband to the Lord. Elizabeth wrote her prayers on pieces of paper and taped them to the closet walls, and she spent regular time in this place of prayer fighting for God's intervention in what looked to most like another marriage doomed to divorce.

I won't spoil the movie for you if you haven't seen it yet, but as I sat and watched it for the first time—along with Priscilla and the rest of my family—I was grateful for the message being displayed on the screen. Prayer really does change things, but far too few of us use it as the powerful tool it is. We don't give our worries to God and thank Him in our times of prayer. Instead, we complain and throw a pity party. But Paul instructs us to set our worries aside and go to God in a spirit of thanksgiving.

What if you have nothing to be thankful for, you ask? Then be thankful for what God is going to do, because nothing is impossible with Him (Luke 1:37). Be thankful that He's given you the opportunity to pray. Be thankful that He brought you and your spouse together way back when. Be thankful for the plans He has for you. Be thankful that He has prompted you to pray. Be thankful for His Word and His promises. Just be thankful, because it is in gratitude that you express trust in God and His ways.

As you set worry aside, replacing it with gratitude, you are exercising faith. In that faith, you then make your requests known to God. Be as specific as you want to be. Sometimes it's good to be specific, because when God answers that prayer, you know that only He could have done it. And that grows your faith even more.

If your spouse hasn't been communicating with you as much as you would like, then ask for that. If he or she has grown distant, then ask God to restore the passion that was once there, and even make it burn deeper. If you are married to a slob and it drives you mad, then ask God to zero in on that. He may change the problem, or He may change you in how you deal with the problem. But one way or another, He will answer your prayer when it is coupled with a heart of thanksgiving and trust.

> *As you set worry aside, replacing it with gratitude, you are exercising faith.*

Now, God doesn't always answer our prayers the way we want Him to. Sometimes He is trying to teach us something through waiting, but He will give us the ability to wait or receive a no answer when we have committed the issue at hand to Him in prayer.

Too often in our marriages, we react to our spouses out of our emotions rather than looking to God to see how we should respond. How many times have you said or done something to your spouse that you later regretted? The Lord could have prevented that if you had gone to Him in prayer for wisdom on how to respond. Far too many spouses seek to be the Holy Spirit to their mates rather than leaving room for the *real* Holy Spirit to work. When you see a need for growth in your spouse, take that need to the Lord and ask the Holy Spirit to guide, correct, and teach him or her. Most of the time, God will point out things in your own life that you can improve as well, which will help the situation.

Make it a point to begin every single day bathing your marriage in prayer. It doesn't have to be long, but it has to be authentic. Thank God for your mate and pray for His will to be manifest in your mate's life. Pray that your mate will grow spiritually and emotionally and even be healthy physically. Ask the Lord to surround your mate with godly relationships and clearly reveal His purpose for him or her. Also ask God to give your mate a desire to steward your family resources well and also to lead, learn, and love you. Ask God to bring greater passion and spontaneity into your sex life. And ask Him to help your mate love Him with all his or her heart, soul, and mind.

> ✤✤✤✤✤
>
> *Your marriage is a spiritual covenant and the target of Satan's daily attacks.*
>
> ✤✤✤✤✤

Then after you have prayed all that and more, turn your prayers toward yourself each day, asking the Lord to do the same things in you. Ask Him to give you a gentle spirit toward your spouse. Ask Him to cause you both to be friends and lovers, adventurers together, and prayer partners for each other, and to reveal anything in your relationship that you can improve on. Ask God to give you both a sensitivity to seek Him before reacting to each other.

You may be saying, "But, Tony, that's a lot to pray every day!" Well, I'm not done. Your marriage is a spiritual covenant and the target of Satan's daily attacks. Would you say it would be too much for any group of soldiers on the battlefield to set up defenses and offenses against their enemy every day? Neither is it too much for you to bathe your marriage in prayer daily.

After you have prayed through these suggestions and anything else you add to it on an ongoing basis, be sure to cover your marriage with the blood of Jesus Christ for protection from the Enemy's darts, schemes, tricks, temptations, and the like. Ask the Lord to station His angels around you and your mate to stand guard against anything the Devil sends to destroy you, and rebuke Satan (in Jesus's name) from any harm he intends toward you.

But your prayers for your marriage shouldn't end there. Keep your relationship at the forefront of your mind, and when you begin to feel frustrated with your spouse for anything, go to God *first* before you react. Ask for His insight on

Make prayer a habit and the first line of both defense and offense in your marriage, and watch what God does.

how you should respond, and for His intervention if you believe your spouse is wrong. Make prayer a habit and the first line of both defense and offense in your marriage, and watch what God does. You will be amazed at how quickly He can heal hearts, revive love, and deepen respect and attachment when you operate in your marriage according to His spiritual hierarchy and covering.

The Peace of God

You may not get every single prayer answered exactly as you requested, because God's ways are higher than our ways, and we have to trust that He knows best (Isaiah 55:8–9). But in Philippians 4:7, Paul tells us one thing we can count on when we pray this way: "The peace of God, which surpasses all comprehension, will guard your hearts and your minds in Christ Jesus." We'll get peace. I know a few marriages that could stand some peace, and maybe yours as well? Peace is the calm in the midst of the storm. Peace is not a promise that you will have no more problems; it's a promise that your problems will no longer have you. Scripture punctuates this promise in the book of Isaiah: "The steadfast of mind You will keep in perfect peace, because he trusts in You" (26:3).

What used to bother you, agitate you, irritate you, and cause you to react to your spouse in an unloving way will no longer do so, because you will have the peace that surpasses understanding. How is it possible to live with a miserable spouse and still be full of joy and peace? Because the peace God gives is beyond what we can explain. This peace stands as a sentry—a soldier—to "guard" your heart and mind. When Paul wrote that word, he used a military term. Sometimes marriage can feel like war, can't it? But when you commit your marriage to prayer according to the principles outlined in Paul's letter from prison, God will keep the epicenter of your emotions calm, because He Himself will *guard* them with His peace.

All worry is related to our thoughts. All anger is related to our thoughts. In fact, all emotions are related to our thoughts. The reason we worry is because we are thinking wrongly. That's why Paul zeroed in on our thoughts following his insights on prayer:

> Finally, brethren, whatever is true, whatever is honorable, whatever is right, whatever is pure, whatever is lovely, whatever is of good repute, if there is any excellence and if anything worthy of praise, dwell [think] on these things. The things you have learned and received and heard and seen in me, practice these things, and the God of peace will be with you. (Philippians 4:8–9)

You cannot change the way you feel until you change the way you think, because what controls the way you think will determine the way you feel. If you feel worried about your marriage, it is because you are thinking thoughts of worry about your marriage. If you feel frustrated about your spouse, it is because you are thinking thoughts of frustration about your spouse. You are thinking about the wrong set of circumstances. Paul reminds us that we are to think about things that are lovely, good, excellent, pure, and worthy of praise. Feed your mind these thoughts about your marriage, and you will receive the long-term benefit that God promises in verse 9: "The God of peace will be with you."

Notice the difference between verse 7 and verse 9. When you develop an authentic and consistent prayer life (according to verse 7), you get the peace of God. But when you couple that with right thoughts resulting in right actions (according to verse 9), you get the God of peace. Paul flipped it because the two are not the same. The peace of God is given to you as a means of covering your amplified emotions or stabilizing your reactions. This is good and it is critical, but when you get the "God of peace," you get that plus a whole lot more. You have deepened your relationship and intimacy with the omniscient, omnipotent, sovereign, compassionate, loving God. His attributes become manifest around you in such a way that you experience Him like never before.

A large percentage of our prayers are what I call short-term prayers. They are about solutions to problems we can see. But we serve a long-term God who knows what is best for us in the long run. God measures what He is going to do for us and when He will do it based on our long-term good and in alignment with His plans for our destiny and growth. As I said before, God may not answer every prayer you have for your marriage the way you want Him to. In fact, He may even ask you to wait. And I hear your complaint, "But, Tony, I can't wait any longer."

> *You cannot change the way you feel until you change the way you think, because what controls the way you think will determine the way you feel.*

And you are right. You can't wait if you are frustrated, emotionally spent, hurt, and living without self-control. But you can wait if you have peace. If you have His peace, you can hang in there for God to do the work in both your spouse and you that is necessary for a vibrant, healthy relationship.

Taking Prayer Further

Prayer is relational communion with God. It is earthly permission for heavenly intervention, and it is a powerful tool in the hands of any spouse. But the Bible teaches a certain parameter for prayer in marriage that can make it all the more potent: combining prayer with sexual fasting. Fasting is giving up a craving in the body because you have a deeper need in the spirit. Next to food, and sometimes even greater than the desire for food, is the craving a person often has for physical intimacy. Knowing this as our designer, God doesn't skip this subject in His Word. The principle is laid out plainly for us in 1 Corinthians, where Paul penned these words:

> Stop depriving one another, except by agreement for a time, so that you may devote yourselves to prayer, and come together again so that Satan will not tempt you because of your lack of self-control. (7:5)

The context of this verse is important because Paul had been speaking in the first four verses of this chapter specifically about sexual intimacy. In those verses he specifically stated that neither a husband nor a wife should neglect to fulfill the "duty" of sexual involvement with each other. Sex is a critical component of marriage that not only provides pleasure but also releases complex biochemicals that, as science has demonstrated, bind

———— ✤✤✤✤✤ ————

Our Lord didn't design sex simply as something to do as a hobby.

———— ✤✤✤✤✤ ————

two people together, arousing desires of protection, loyalty, and more. Our Lord didn't design sex simply as something to do as a hobby. When carried out in the covenantal confines of a marriage, sex is the glue (from a biochemical standpoint) that keeps couples united.

However, there is one time our Lord instructs us to go without marital sexual relations, and that is when we are giving up physical intimacy to gain spiritual intimacy with regard to prayer. Please notice what Paul wrote: You are to do this when you are, as a couple, in "agreement." In other words, it takes two to make this decision, since as a Christian husband or a Christian wife, sexual relations are now concerned with pleasing the other person, not just yourself (verses 3–4).

The Purpose of Prayer and Sexual Fasting

Sexual fasting seeks to deepen the spiritual intimacy of a couple as the two go before the Lord in agreement and prayer. It is designed to reach the root of any issues the couple is facing, but it can also be used in pursuit of an even greater spiritual level or breakthrough that the couple may be desiring. Let's say, for instance, that the wife in a marriage was offered a new job that will require significant hours away from the home yet is entirely in alignment with her gifts, skills, and passion. Not only that, but the job advances God's kingdom and appears to have come to her through God's ordained plans. Even so, the acceptance of this job will surely affect the daily dynamics of the home. Prayer is one way to seek God's guidance and confirmation on this decision, but prayer coupled with sexual fasting deepens this pursuit even more. It provides an atmosphere of urgency that opens the doorway for clarity and agreement to occur.

Sexual fasting can also occur when a couple is in disagreement or in conflict, and both parties desire to overcome the existing issues but do not see a tangible way to do so. At these times when a couple has grown distant, sexual intimacy may not be occurring on a regular basis. But by agreeing to set a time for sexual fasting with the intention of joint prayer, the couple has taken a proactive approach to healing rather than a reactionary approach to conflict. Keep in mind that after the established and agreed-upon time has passed, the Bible urges a couple to unite again in sexual intimacy.

Much of what creates conflict in a marriage is merely a symptom of a deeper problem. While you may think it's a personality difference or a values difference, the core of the battle comes from the garden where Satan brought about disruption by getting each party to vacate their respective roles and rebel. When couples fail to deal with the spiritual root while merely focusing on the fruit, they set themselves up for a cyclical storm.

Sexual fasting with the intention of deepening your prayer life as a couple exists to get to the spiritual agitation that is producing the physical confrontation. It is designed to address the underlying causes in

> *Much of what creates conflict in a marriage is merely a symptom of a deeper problem.*

the spiritual realm that are manifesting the conflict in the physical realm. Everything physical is rooted in something spiritual. The problem today in so many marriages is that couples focus entirely on the physical symptoms of an issue, trying to micromanage each other, rather than dealing with the heart and spiritual core of what is causing the conflict.

Over the years I've had the honor of serving as the chaplain for the Dallas Cowboys during different seasons. Some of the highlights of those times were during the Tom Landry years when the Cowboys dominated so much of professional football and went to the Super Bowl a number of times. Now what does this have to do with sexual fasting? Hold on, I'm getting there. You may not realize that the entire week before the Super Bowl, players on both teams (whether married or not) are to abstain from sex.[2] In essence, they fast from sex.

Sexual fasting demonstrates to God that you are asking to meet Him at a deeper level.

Why? Because coaches have learned in the past that when players engage in sex leading up to a game, it can drain them of both their energy and their focus. For this and other reasons, all players have to observe not only a curfew but also a no-visitors rule that entire week. Coaches have been known to sneak into players' rooms with flashlights at any time of night to make sure they're abiding by these parameters.

Now if the NFL coaches get better focus from their players in the big game when those players abstain from sex, I imagine God gets much deeper focus from married couples in prayer when they also, in agreement, abstain from sex for a time. When God chose to visit the Israelites in the closeness of His presence, He instructed the men and women to abstain from sex. He wanted their deepest attachment and attention (Exodus 19:9–15). When He called His people to a solemn assembly—a sacred time of spiritual renewal with Him—He instructed the bridegroom and bride to leave their chambers, which is another way to push the pause button on sex (Joel 2:16).

Whether your marriage is languishing in confusion, distance, or conflict, or you and your mate are seeking God's hand of blessing, favor, guidance, or manifestation in a specific area, sexual fasting demonstrates to God that you are asking to meet Him at a deeper level.

When you engage in sex as a couple, you discover how to be in tune with each other physically. When you engage in mutually agreed-upon sexual fasting for the purpose of prayer, you discover how to be in tune with each other even more deeply spiritually. As a result, a greater experience of God will produce greater growth in your relationship.

First Peter 3:7 reminds us of a very sobering truth: There's more to having your prayers heard and answered than merely saying them. We read, "You husbands in the same way, live with your wives in an understanding way, as with someone weaker, since she is a woman; and show her honor as a fellow heir of the grace of life, so that your prayers will not be hindered." When there is disunity in your relationship, God is kept at bay. Even with regard to your prayers.

The principles we are looking at in this book go hand in hand. Living with your spouse in a spirit of honor and unity will open the pathway to a more effective prayer life. Prayer is a powerful weapon in the war room of marriage, but it is a weapon that must be wielded wisely, with grace, humility, honor for each other, understanding, and—when agreed upon—sexual fasting.

9

✣✣✣✣✣✣

RESTORATION

ONE OF THE STRONGHOLDS that many married couples struggle with is the area of forgiveness. I call unforgiveness a stronghold simply because so many spouses have come to me stating that this is one area in their marriage that they don't think they can overcome. Anytime you look at a situation that you believe to be irreversible, even though God says otherwise, you are dealing with a stronghold. You cannot use human methodology to overcome a stronghold. Only spiritual weapons can defeat spiritual strongholds.

We know, based on our previous look at Satan's attack in the garden, that a spiritual being, Satan, initiated the deterioration of the first marriage and family (Adam and Eve's). A fallen angel disrupted the first home by causing spiritual fractures that led to relational fractures. Keep in mind, it wasn't the relationship between Adam and Eve that first went bad but their relationship with God, which then worked itself out in the human environment.

Just as an interfering angel of darkness was the root cause of the first marriage suffering a breakup, Satan and his desire to destroy the home is the same root cause for every family breakup. Forgiveness is a critical element of a healthy marriage, because when you and I are living in a state of unforgiveness toward someone else, God says He will not live in a state of relational forgiveness with us (Matthew 6:15). Once the spiritual relationship with God is broken or damaged because of ongoing sin, we limit the experiential presence and power of God in our lives and our marriages.

There are several vehicles through which Satan is given an opportunity to bring a stronghold into your home, one of which is unresolved anger. In Ephesians 4:26–27 we read, "Be angry, and yet do not sin; do not let the sun go down on your anger, and do not give the devil an opportunity." Paul started out here by stating that it's okay to be angry. In fact, he plainly said, "Be angry." If your spouse has sinned against you in some way, or you have sinned against your spouse, you or your spouse has every right to be angry. Anger at sin is valid. Scripture tells us that the Lord is angry at wicked people every day (Psalm 7:11; Romans 1:18). If wrong has been done against you, you have the right to be angry. But what you do not have the right to do is let your anger go unresolved, or to sin in your anger.

The prolonged buildup of anger in a marriage often provides Satan with a steering wheel to turn a problem into a stronghold. Unaddressed anger that has been allowed to accumulate over time will open the door for spiritual warfare to wreak havoc on your home.

Many, if not most, of the problems between couples stem from unresolved anger over something done in the past, or an ongoing pattern. Unresolved anger becomes an opportunity for Satan to disrupt your marriage.

One of the worst habits or patterns you can fall into in a marriage is reacting. In conflict, don't react. Don't let your emotions respond impulsively. For example, if you know that whatever you are discussing or doing is going to end up in a conflict, then set a specific time in the future when you will be able to discuss it rationally, without the heat of emotion. If you know that a certain area or subject is especially sensitive for the other person, then create the space to allow those sensitivities to die down before you seek resolution.

Don't leave your spouse in a state of not knowing whether you will address the conflict and anger you are feeling later.

However, don't leave your spouse in a state of not knowing whether you will address the conflict and anger you are feeling later. It may not be possible to resolve the situation that day, but you can set a time when you both know you can communicate with each other about it in an emotionally healthy way.

Far too many couples not only let the sun go down on their anger, but they also let the moon go down on their wrath, and before they know it, an entire decade has gone down on their marriage. Some couples even take their anger to the grave. In fact, unresolved anger can linger past the grave. The story is told of a man who was at the Super Bowl with an empty seat next to him. Someone sitting near him asked whether anyone was attending the game with him.

The man answered, "Well, my wife used to come to all the games with me, but she died."

The other man asked if he had no other friends to come with him, to which the widower replied, "No, they are all at the funeral."

There are a number of problems with unresolved anger—or a lack of forgiveness. One is that those around you often have to pay for someone else's sin, whether they are coworkers, your children, or even your spouse. When you live with unforgiveness, that bitterness and contempt seep into other relationships, perhaps through unkind words, a lack of love, or any number of other ways.

Suppose you were at a restaurant, and the waiter gave you a bill for $3,500—the total of all the receipts of everyone in the restaurant. Would you pay it? Of course not, because you shouldn't have to pay for what other people ate. Likewise, it's not fair to make those around you pay for what someone else may have done to you. Sometimes spouses make each other pay for what their parents did to them. At other times, parents make children or friends pay for how their spouses treat them. Unforgiveness is a sore that spreads infection throughout the body when left unchecked.

We all know what happens to a sore that goes untreated: It festers, and bacteria begins to grow. If you got a cut on your arm but didn't clean it or care for it, in time that wound would start to ooze with pus. It would become red around the edges and warm to the touch. In time, you wouldn't even be able to touch it because it would hurt so much. Soon the bacteria would reach your bloodstream, and what began as a cut would now be a dangerous, life-threatening staph infection.

But even if you covered that wound so that no one could see the oozing pus, and you went about your normal routine, the people around you would definitely feel your reaction if they so much as lightly grazed you while passing by. If someone bumped into your now-throbbing wound, you would jerk your arm back in pain and might even lash out at the person in response. Your reaction wouldn't be reflective of what that person did, because what he or she did was simply an accident. But that person would receive the full venting of your pain simply because you did not treat your wound so that it would heal. In fact, if you continued walking around with a festering sore, you'd be highly sensitive and reactive to anything that came in contact with it.

— ✤✤✤✤✤ —

When the wounds in our hearts are left untreated, they rot, thus producing residual pain in other areas of our lives.

— ✤✤✤✤✤ —

Unforgiveness is like an untreated wound in the soul. It boils over with the heat of bitterness and sets a cycle in motion where small marital scuffles become large wars (Matthew 18:23–34). When the wounds in our hearts are left untreated, they rot, thus producing residual pain in other areas of our lives. As a result, we become highly sensitive and reactive to the actions, words, and nonactions of our spouses. The slightest brush or offense from our mates—even if they didn't mean anything harmful at all—evokes a harsh reaction. We may lash out, accuse, blame, cry, or say and do things we later regret. All the while, our spouses are caught off guard by our reactions. To overcome unforgiveness, we need to treat our wounds and let them heal.

Release and Replace

It's far easier to talk about forgiving someone than to actually do it. Forgiveness is a beautiful word when you are on the receiving end of it. It becomes an ugly word when you are the one having to give it. One of the better analogies I have for forgiveness is comparing it to ejecting a CD, DVD, or Blu-ray Disc from a player. These players are tremendous machines that give us the ability to watch or listen to something time and time again. But one thing is true: We can never put in a new disc until we take the first one out. We can't play two discs simultaneously. We must eject the first disc to play the second.

Likewise in marriage, you can't experience a healthy, thriving relationship with your spouse if you keep replaying whatever it is he or she did to anger you. You have to eject that offense and replace it with love. The only way to do that is to release your spouse from what he or she did to hurt you. You have to turn the offense over to God and replace your thoughts of anger, hurt, and pain with thoughts of thanksgiving—gratitude that God has given you the faith and ability to be released from the stronghold of unforgiveness.

Biblical forgiveness is the decision to no longer credit an offense against your spouse with a view of enacting vengeance. It means you release your spouse from a debt owed to you as well as the blame he or she may deserve. Forgiveness is first and foremost a decision. It doesn't begin with an emotion. It is not contingent on how you feel about your spouse, but rather it is a choice to no longer blame your spouse for an offense.

First Corinthians 13:5 details this for us in a most straightforward way: Biblical love "keeps no record of wrongs" (NIV). Biblical love doesn't justify wrong, nor does it ignore wrong, excuse it, or pretend it doesn't exist. All of those types of responses to wrongdoing would lead to enablement. Rather, biblical love acknowledges and addresses the wrong and then forgives and releases it while keeping no record of it. I've been in counseling sessions with some couples who bring up things that were said or done not years ago but decades ago. When I hear this, and it happens far too often, I sigh inside because I know that the roots of bitterness and unforgiveness run deep. I also know that Satan has been allowed to

The arguments become so toxic and volatile in their language and tone that they produce no good but drive a deeper wedge of division into the marriage.

run the show in that marriage, making the stronghold ever more formidable to tear down.

You may be surprised at the advice I give when strongholds run that deep. I've seen it work in countless marriages, and I believe in its effectiveness because it addresses the unresolved anger that often feeds our failure to forgive. Often what happens in marriages that are clouded by unresolved anger is that the arguments become so toxic and volatile in their language and tone that they produce no good but drive a deeper wedge of division into the marriage. So this is what I propose if you have found yourself in a marriage with unresolved anger:

1. *Say something and do something every day that expresses value to your spouse.* This might be a note, an unexpected phone call, a nonsexual hug, or a time of cuddling. Married couples are good at doing big things on big days like birthdays, anniversaries, or Valentine's Day, but what we often neglect to do is cultivate and maintain in small but consistent ways a recognition that we value each other.

2. *Pray daily for each other and with each other.* I don't mean just saying a blessing before a meal. This is a specific time you come together, holding hands or holding each other, kneeling beside the bed or in your closet, or sitting on the couch—it doesn't matter—and pray aloud for your marriage. This is not a time to hash out differences by bringing them before the Lord in prayer, but rather a time to pray that God will bless your spouse and that He will bless the two of you together with His grace and mercy.

3. *Date regularly.* Too many marriages get caught up in drudgery or routine, and spouses lose the fun they once had. By "date" I mean pick a place and something fun to do. That doesn't mean grabbing dinner at a restaurant because neither of you feel like cooking, and you have to eat anyhow. At a minimum, do something fun together every other week, if not more often.

4. *Set an agreed-upon time weekly where you sit down together and allow the spouse who holds the unresolved anger to vent.* This means that the other spouse agrees not to argue, defend, or tune out the venting. It's

like when we have an upset stomach because we have bacteria inside us, and we feel better when we are able to throw up.

Far too many married couples never give each other the freedom to get rid of the bacteria by speaking. I don't mean couples don't yell at each other—they do all the time. But this is a set time every week where one spouse is allowed to vent his or her pain without the fear of being shut down. Turn off the television and your phone. The other spouse must agree to give his or her undivided attention to the venting spouse. If nagging is a problem in your marriage, this will solve it. Because when you agree to listen, the spouse who is venting also agrees not to bring up these issues during the week—unless something is time sensitive.

I've used this four-step approach with countless couples, and before long, that one hour a week turns into thirty minutes and then fifteen minutes—and then it's not even needed at all.

So much of what we harbor against each other as married couples is stuffed down and then thrown at each other in nagging or fights in which we don't feel heard or validated. Healing comes from a place of understanding and validation. When you allow your spouse the freedom to communicate what has pained him or her, and you validate that pain without becoming defensive or saying your spouse is wrong to feel it, you will be amazed at how quickly healing and forgiveness will come.

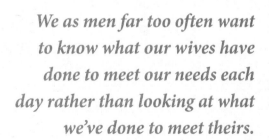

We as men far too often want to know what our wives have done to meet our needs each day rather than looking at what we've done to meet theirs.

When you implement all four of these steps simultaneously, you will see and experience healing in your marriage. Doing these things from an authentic place of relational connection allows you to begin putting more deposits into your spouse than withdrawals. Too many spouses seek to make more withdrawals from their relationships than deposits. Men, in particular, have the propensity to come home after work tired and look for what their wives have done for them—the dinner, the house, children, even if their wives are working full-time too. We as men far too often want to know what our wives have done to meet our needs each day rather than looking at what we have done to meet theirs. As a result, our wives constantly have to make withdrawals from their love accounts, and so their accounts run empty.

If that describes you, husbands, then don't be upset if there's nothing in the bank at night. Both spouses need to make more deposits than withdrawals in their relationship. When you wake up in the morning, and as you go about your day, ask yourself what you can do to make a deposit in your spouse's life. It doesn't have to be huge, but it does need to be consistent. Life has a way of dictating the withdrawals—they'll come whether you seek them out or not. So what you need to do as a spouse is look for ways to make deposits.

The problems in our marriages are spiritual at their core, so the solutions to overcoming them must be spiritual as well.

Otherwise your spouse's account will bounce, and when it comes time for forgiveness to be granted, you will lack the emotional depth and relational harmony to grant it easily. Love must be proactive if it's to be ongoing.

The story is told of a couple who had been fighting so much that they were on their way to divorce court. A counselor told them they should take up a mutual hobby to save their marriage. The couple thought it was worth a try, so they chose duck hunting. One thing they knew they needed was a good duck-hunting dog. So this couple spent time and money securing the best duck-hunting dog they could find.

Finally the day arrived when they were to go duck hunting together. They stood along the banks and hunted all day long. Much to their disappointment, they never got one single duck. Frustrated and weary at the end of a long day, the husband said, "We have got to be doing something wrong. We haven't even come close to catching a duck."

To which his wife replied, "Well, throw the dog up higher. He's not high enough to grab hold of the duck!"

That's what a lot of couples are doing. They are trying to get a dog to do what a gun was meant to do, and all the while they're wondering why they aren't getting any ducks. The reason is because a dog is not the right weapon. A dog is ancillary. It's nice to have a dog when you go duck hunting, but the dog alone won't get the duck. You need firepower to bring that duck down, and then the dog can do his job.

I'll say it again: The problems in our marriages are spiritual at their core, so the solutions to overcoming them must be spiritual as well. You can take a vacation and probably improve your marriage a bit. You can buy a new ring and possibly improve your marriage some. You can get a new house and enjoy some moments of peace. But none of that is going to last, because none of it is based in the spiritual realm. Only when you commit your conflict to prayer, healthy communication, humility, and forgiveness will you experience the power to overcome strongholds in your marriage.

But What If My Spouse Doesn't Apologize?

What about those times when your spouse isn't sorry—how do you forgive then? Unfortunately this is a reality in marriages as well. That's why I want to discuss briefly the importance of unilateral forgiveness in marriage. Unilateral forgiveness is when you choose to forgive your spouse even if he or she has not asked for it and may not even have repented. Essentially you are granting your mate forgiveness on your own—unilaterally—without his or her involvement.

Why would you grant forgiveness to someone who doesn't want it, has not asked for it, and certainly may not deserve it? The reason you grant unilateral forgiveness is not to set *your spouse* free to move on but

> *The reason you grant unilateral forgiveness is not to set your spouse free to move on but to set yourself free.*

to set *yourself* free. It's so that you can keep going. Unilateral forgiveness keeps you from being bound to something the other person may never get right. This is what God did on the cross by "not counting [our] trespasses against [us]" (2 Corinthians 5:19). Unilateral forgiveness also releases God to deal directly with your spouse regarding this offense.

If you watch sports at all, you know that when a player fouls another player, such as in basketball, the referee calls the foul. As a result, the player who was fouled gets to shoot from the free-throw line or gets to throw the ball back into play. However, if the player who was fouled decides to fight back against the one who fouled him, fouls are called on both players, and the player who was originally fouled is penalized as well. Unilateral forgiveness in a marriage releases God to work on your spouse to either correct or bring him or her to repentance. When you stand in the way with your unforgiveness, you are drawing God's attention back to you, and now He has to respond to your sin as well.

When you are not willing to unilaterally forgive, it is you who are held hostage, not the other person. You cannot control what happened to you; you can only control your response to it, so that's where you need to focus. I remember one time when I had to unilaterally forgive. It was a minor thing in the big scheme of life, but to me it was a real challenge. It involved a hit-and-run accident where a driver hit my car but left without giving me any insurance documentation. The driver didn't apologize and didn't even stop to see if I was okay or if I needed help. He or she just banged into my car and then left.

Forgiveness is crucial for any marriage to thrive. But if that forgiveness is conditional, it is not couched in the love of God.

In the days and weeks that passed, each time I looked at my mangled car, I felt frustrated, angry, and a bunch of other unsanctified emotions. It wasn't my fault that the other driver hit me. But the longer I delayed getting my car fixed just because I didn't think it was my fault or my responsibility to pay for the damage, the longer it took my wound to heal. I had to fix the damage myself in order to get the freedom to move on. I had to unilaterally forgive, or it would be me being held hostage to what the other person had done. Unilateral forgiveness doesn't just release the other person; it releases you.

Forgiveness is crucial for any marriage to thrive. But if that forgiveness is conditional, it is not couched in the love of God. Jesus Christ died for our sins and asked His Father to forgive us while doing it Himself. He didn't wait to give us His gift of mercy and grace until we got our act together or came humbly to him with flowers or chocolates. Forgiveness is probably the greatest gift you can give your spouse, but it's also the greatest gift you can give yourself. Forgiving opens your marriage to the flow of God's favor to you, and through you, to your spouse.

10

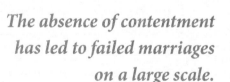

RESOURCES

ONE OF THE GREATEST CONTRIBUTORS to financial health in a marriage is contentment. In fact, the apostle Paul called it a "secret." The absence of contentment has led to failed marriages on a large scale. Much of this arises from a desire to live above an available budget and thus accrue debt, which leads to financial strain on the relationship. Another aspect comes from a dependency on the two-income home. Without negating a wife's value and contributions in the workplace, we have to keep in mind that there are seasons for everything. There are times when having two incomes doesn't tax the makeup and dynamics of the home. But there are other times when it contributes to the devolution of family health and harmony. When married couples do not give themselves the option of living on one salary, or perhaps combining one salary with a part-time endeavor, they put themselves under the strain of meeting excessive demands.

> *The absence of contentment has led to failed marriages on a large scale.*

The dual pressure to keep up with the Joneses—buying things we don't need with money we don't have to impress people we don't know—and pursue careers at the expense of our relationships keeps us in a state of discontentment and facilitates marital stress and conflict.

In or outside of marriage, you will find very few people today who are content. Advertising and marketing in our culture always dangles another carrot in front of us to get us to be more, spend more, and do more. With technology at our fingertips, we have a greater opportunity to spend, spend, spend like never before. Just one click, and what we are looking at on our computer screens can arrive on our doorsteps the next day. It's difficult to remain content when we are continually being told what else we need to make ourselves happy, healthy, or good-looking. We can't seem to buy enough stuff to keep our kids happy, and God can't seem to give enough stuff to keep His kids happy either.

A lack of contentment doesn't seem new, though. I'm sure contentment wasn't easy in Bible times either. The reason I'm sure is because Paul called it a "secret." In describing the art of being satisfied, he used a word that literally means not many people know about it. Here's what Paul had to say in his letter to the church at Philippi:

> I know how to get along with humble means, and I also know how
> to live in prosperity; in any and every circumstance I have learned the
> secret of being filled and going hungry, both of having abundance
> and suffering need. (Philippians 4:12)

Paul's words ring like our contemporary wedding vows in many ways: "For richer, for poorer; in sickness and in health." When a couple gets married, in essence, they are pledging to be content with each other, no matter what situation they face.

Yet that is not what happens. When financial trials come, contentment is often the first thing to fly out the window of unmet expectations. Like thermometers, marriages go up and down based on the temperature of the bank account. But that is not what Paul was referring to when he said he knew the secret of contentment. Paul was speaking of the true meaning of the word: "to be contained." Contentment means to have the resources available to handle whatever we are dealing with. In other words, we have enough for what we need at any given time, whether that enough is a lot or a little.

How do you know when you are content? You know when you are at ease regardless of what is going on around you. Contentment means being at rest, thankful and grateful for whatever situation you find yourself in. You can always know someone's contentment level by whether he or she is complaining more or being grateful. If complaints are in control, there is no contentment. If gratitude is the dominant presence, contentment is there.

More money doesn't automatically translate into contentment. One of the happiest seasons in marriage for a lot of couples was when they started out without a dime to their names but knew that their love could take on the world. Two decades later, and the apartment has turned into a house, two new leases have replaced the used car, and a trip to the relatives is now a trip to the sea. These same couples bicker and fight about finances because a lack of contentment has set in. There is always a bigger

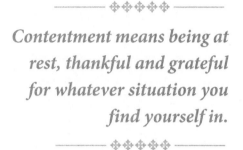

Contentment means being at rest, thankful and grateful for whatever situation you find yourself in.

house to be had, a newer car to drive, nicer clothes to buy, and better places to go. It seems as if the more exposed people are to what they can do, the more they want to do, buy, or be.

Paul's secret could save many marriages if it were learned and applied. Life ebbs and flows. Sometimes you are up financially, and sometimes things will be tight. A couple in a kingdom marriage allows Paul's secret to rule their hearts and minds. They value what is most important in life: their relationship with God and with each other.

Stewardship Principles in Marriage

A number of couples I've counseled acknowledged to me that they have separate bank accounts. The wife keeps her money in one account, and the husband keeps his money in another. And while that may be fine for the distribution of funds, it creates a misunderstanding about whose funds they are in the first place. After all, "the earth is the LORD's, and all it contains" (Psalm 24:1). Embracing this reality about our resources can not only alleviate a large portion of marital financial conflict, but it can also turn what might be a difficult area in the relationship into a joyous one.

Since financial issues still rank as one of the top causes for marital discord in our country today and are often a leading cause of divorce, I'd like to look at cultivating a kingdom perspective on our resources. Let's learn what it truly means to live as faithful couples stewarding our resources for the Lord.

In an 1863 speech calling for a national day of prayer and fasting, Abraham Lincoln said,

> We have been the recipients of the choicest bounties of Heaven. We have been preserved, these many years, in peace and prosperity. We have grown in numbers, wealth and power, as no other nation has ever grown. But we have forgotten God. We have forgotten the gracious hand which preserved us in peace, and multiplied and enriched and strengthened us; and we have vainly imagined, in the deceitfulness of our hearts, that all these blessings were produced by some superior wisdom and virtue of our own. Intoxicated with unbroken success, we have become too self-sufficient to feel the necessity of redeeming and preserving grace, too proud to pray to the God that made us![1]

If these words rang true in Abraham Lincoln's day, which they did, how much more are they true today. We are living in a time of unprecedented prosperity. As individuals and families, we have received so much from God. Few of us lack any necessary resource for life and liberty, and many of us are privileged to have the monetary blessings that offer us things like the freedom to choose our possessions, travel,

❖❖❖❖❖

We are living in a time of unprecedented prosperity.

❖❖❖❖❖

and much more. On a large scale, God has provided for our needs, and more, through His unlimited grace.

Not only that, but He sustains the universe and gives us the gift of life each morning. He surrounds us with friends and family and promises us eternal life through His Son. Yet we often forget His gifts and think that life is about us. We squander the time, talents, and treasures He has given us by investing them in our own selfish goals and claiming them for our own personal gain. We forget that the resources the Lord has entrusted to us as couples are kingdom resources He owns, and they are to be used to advance His Kingdom agenda on earth.

What if we as couples were to live as if we truly recognized that God owns everything (Psalm 24:1), and our job is simply to manage and invest His resources for His purposes? How would that change our mind-set toward our bills, what we buy, where we eat, and what we do? How would we use our time differently? And how much joy and freedom would we experience if we remembered that our legacy in life and our reward in eternity depend not on our bank accounts but on the lives God touches through us?

In the parable found in Luke 19:11–27, Jesus was the nobleman who left his land to receive his kingdom. We read in verses 12–13, "So He said, 'A nobleman went to a distant country to receive a kingdom for himself, and then return. And he called ten of his slaves, and gave them ten minas and said to them, 'Do business with this until I come back.'"

The parable goes on to discuss what each person did with the money and how the nobleman responded to each. Carrying this over to Christ in the present age, we know that after Jesus died on the cross and rose from the dead, He ascended to heaven, where He waits until the appointed time to return and set up His kingdom on earth. In the meantime, He has entrusted us with some of His resources to manage until He returns. We are to "do business with this until [He comes] back."

The first point of any business is to understand who owns the assets. In Psalm 50:10–12, God reminds us that "every beast of the forest is Mine, the cattle on a thousand hills. I know every bird of the mountains, and everything that moves in the field is Mine. If I were hungry I would not tell you, for the world is Mine, and all it contains." In other words, God owns it all. God, as creator, owns everything in creation, including every material possession you have, every dollar in your bank account, and everything you will eventually buy. He has appointed us as human beings to be stewards or managers of His resources. They are not my resources, nor are they your resources. Therefore, they cannot be merely the husband's resources or the wife's resources. God owns them all. When we truly recognize this reality, we can loosen our grip on all the "things" in our lives and increase our generosity toward God and others. We can lessen the possessiveness and feelings of entitlement in our marriages. This changes our mind-set from a me-versus-you mentality to an us-under-God mentality.

Revelation 4:11 casts a revealing light on stewardship: "Worthy are You, our Lord and our God, to receive glory and honor and power; for You created all things, and because of Your will they existed, and were created." All things exist for God's will, whether that be our time, our talents, or our treasures. We exist for Him. So when you feel a tug-of-war occurring between you and your spouse regarding how your resources are spent, you are ignoring the real tug-of-war that should take place between you

> *The first point of any business is to understand who owns the assets.*

and the Lord. He is the owner of all you have and claim, so His perspective on how to use it would be the wisest perspective to gain and apply in your marriage. After all, when you and I are one day gone, what will happen to all of the things we tried so hard to accumulate? Job said, "Naked I came from my mother's womb, and naked I shall return there. The LORD gave and the LORD has taken away. Blessed be the name of the LORD" (Job 1:21).

We are reminded in the book of James that although we commit a lot of our time to making plans, producing growth, and simply working, God has the final say about all that we do:

> Come now, you who say, "Today or tomorrow we will go to such and such a city, and spend a year there and engage in business and make a profit." Yet you do not know what your life will be like tomorrow. You are just a vapor that appears for a little while and then vanishes away. Instead, you ought to say, "If the Lord wills, we will live and also do this or that." (4:13–15)

Do you control your own destiny? Do you control your own income? Answering those questions correctly will cause you to be a better steward of all God has given you as a married couple. Prosperity comes only by His grace, because life itself is a gift. Therefore, we are to honor God with what we have been given.

In Isaiah 14, we have a somber reminder of what can happen when we choose not to honor God with what we have been given and instead seek a shared-ownership provision. God is the creator and sustainer of all things. When Satan tried to make himself like God, the Lord humbled him, kicked him out of heaven, and sentenced him to eternal punishment. Pride motivated Satan's claim to God's power and own-

ership. Pride also motivates our desire to claim ownership over the gifts God has given us rather than acting as faithful, responsible, and generous stewards.

The Responsibility of Stewardship

God has generously given us everything we need to live. He has blessed us with resources, time, talents, and abilities, and He expects us to take good care of His gifts. The Lord expects His faithful stewards to invest His gifts in eternal kingdom purposes. In the parable of the stewards found in Luke 19, Jesus spoke of a nobleman who gave each of his servants a different amount of money and commanded them to "do business" while he was gone (verse 13). If we are to "do business" with God's resources in a way that pleases Him and advances His kingdom, we must use in practical ways the time, talents, and treasures He has given us for His glory.

In Matthew 25, Jesus told a parable that's very similar to Luke 19, but with a different emphasis. A man who went on a journey gave differing numbers of talents, or money, to his three slaves (verses 14–30). The catch was that the man gave a different amount to each slave, *according to their different abilities,* to invest and multiply the talents. Though God gives to us all abundantly from His resources and expects us all to manage and multiply the gifts He has given, He doesn't give all of us the same amount of money, time, energy, or abilities. But just as the man who went on a journey judged his slaves' stewardship when he returned, Jesus will hold us accountable for our stewardship when He returns.

The Evaluation of Stewardship

Now that we have examined biblical stewardship, let's look at how God will determine whether we have indeed managed His resources well. How will the Lord evaluate the business we have conducted with His resources?

In 1 Corinthians 3:10–15, Paul compared stewardship to constructing a building. A wise builder takes care to lay a strong foundation and build with proven materials. Likewise, a faithful steward uses the time, talents, and treasures God has given him or her to invest in eternity and store up true gold treasures in heaven rather than spending the God-given resources to live an extravagant lifestyle on earth. Everything we build on earth will be burned up, but the eternal treasures we invest in will endure the fiery test described in this passage of Scripture.

Do you give the Lord and His kingdom your best effort when it comes to using His resources for eternal purposes? Or do you spend your energy to make ends meet or increase your standard of living?

What should motivate your stewardship? You should manage the resources God has given you out of gratitude for His generous grace and provision, and out of reverence, believing that He is holy and will hold you accountable for the way you have managed His gifts. Hebrews 12:28 tells us, "Therefore, since we receive a kingdom which cannot be shaken, let us show gratitude, by which we may offer to God an acceptable service with reverence and awe."

You should manage the resources God has given you out of gratitude for His generous grace and provision.

Thankfulness is to serve as a motivation to steward what God has given you in a way that pleases Him.

The Rewards of Stewardship

God not only gives to us generously from His resources, but He also rewards us when we care for His resources well. However, He will also hold us accountable if we are lazy. Let's examine how God responds to good and poor stewards by returning to the parable mentioned earlier in this chapter and zeroing in on the faithful steward (Luke 19:16-17).

When the master returned from his journey, he called the three stewards and asked them to bring the money they had made. The first steward, who had received one mina, made ten more. In return, the master rewarded the good steward, recognized his accomplishment publicly, and gave him ten cities to rule over. Likewise, when Jesus returns and judges how we have managed His resources, He will reward and recognize His good stewards publicly, and He will give us the appropriate amount of authority in His kingdom.

In verses 18–19 we read that when the second steward came forward and presented his master with five more minas, the master gave him authority over five cities. However, the second steward didn't receive the public recognition— the "well done!"— that the first steward had received.

Finally in verses 20–24, when the third steward brought back the one mina that the master had given him and hadn't made any more money, the master judged him harshly. The worthless steward was lazy, fearful, and selfish. He feared that if he lost the master's one mina, the master would judge him.

Furthermore, the worthless steward was also concerned only with himself and his own interests. He probably spent his time investing his own resources for his

> *We should pray for the Holy Spirit's help to maintain an attitude of gratitude and anticipation of the Lord's return.*

own gain and cared little about his master's interests. As a result, the master severely punished the worthless steward by taking away his one mina and giving it to the faithful steward who already had ten minas.

So how should we, as faithful, responsible stewards, respond to the Lord with what He has entrusted to us as married couples? First, we should remember and live by the words of Hebrews 12:28–29:

> Therefore, since we receive a kingdom which cannot be shaken, let us show gratitude, by which we may offer to God an acceptable service, with reverence and awe; for our God is a consuming fire.

Second, we should pray for the Holy Spirit's help to maintain an attitude of gratitude and anticipation of the Lord's return. We should also pray and actively look for opportunities to use the time, talents, and treasures God has given us for His kingdom.

Third, let's commit to memorizing and meditating on 1 Corinthians 15:58: "Be steadfast, immovable, always abounding in the work of the Lord, knowing that your toil is not in vain in the Lord."

One day, when our mortality catches up with us, our time for investing in God's kingdom will come to an end. So let's use today to make the most of the generous resources God has loaned to us to expand His kingdom and make His glory known to as many people as possible.

Give. Save. Spend.

Are you or your spouse like the seven dwarves who started out each day singing, "I owe, I owe, so off to work I go?" It is no secret that many marriages are drowning in a sea of debt. Debt has become a way of life. It's the newest addiction. Instead of living for the future, we end up paying for the past. The common marriage vow includes the promise to love and cherish "till death do us part." However, we are discovering today that despite our achievements in material success, many couples are only making it as a couple until "debt do us part."

Gross mishandling, misappropriating, or misprioritizing of family funds have led to relational breakdown on a number of levels. Scripture tells us that it is not good for us as believers to live in debt. Proverbs 22:7 says, "The borrower becomes the lender's slave." In fact, God tells us in the book of Luke that if men and women are not able to properly handle the money God gives them, they get cut off from receiving God's other blessings as well (16:10–11).

Debt is not just about money. I don't want you to miss that point, because most of us think that debt *is* just about money. Rather, debt is about your spiritual connection to God. For you and your spouse to fully maximize all that God has created you to do to live out your shared purpose as a kingdom couple, you need to get a handle on your resources. With this in mind, let me close out this chapter on resources with these three simple words: give, save, spend. I give this advice to all couples I counsel in the area of finances. It will help you, too, if you will put it into practice today.

First, *give*. Proverbs 3:9–10 says, "Honor the LORD from your wealth and from the first of all your produce; so your barns will be filled with plenty." Now, I know you are saying that you don't see how you can give to God when you can't even pay all of your bills, but God says that if you will give to Him— honor Him—He will make sure you have enough for what you need.

> To fully maximize all that God has created you to do to live out your shared purpose as a kingdom couple, you need to get a handle on your resources.

I remember when I was in seminary, and Lois and I had young children. We had to take care of a family with only nine hundred dollars a month. Even though the amount we had was small, we always gave ninety dollars to God first as a way of saying that we were trusting Him as our source. We weren't just giving a tithe; we were giving ownership by acknowledging who owned the nine hundred dollars to begin with. Even though things were tight, God was faithful to provide for us at all times.

Next, *save*. A portion of every dollar you earn should go into savings. Egypt was able to not only survive a seven-year famine during Joseph's time, but they were also able to feed people in other lands (Genesis 41:41–57). This is because Joseph instructed the Egyptians to set aside—to save—a portion of every harvest during the seven years leading up to the drought. Life has a way of surprising you sometimes with unexpected expenses. When you make a practice of saving some of your money, you will be prepared for what is in store.

Lastly, *spend*. But spend wisely. Plan your spending. Draw up, agree upon, and stick to a family budget. Play hard and enjoy life but also play smart. God tells us in Proverbs 21:5, "The plans of the diligent lead surely to advantage, but everyone who is hasty comes surely to poverty." There's nothing wrong with spending money or enjoying blessings in life. It just needs to be done with wisdom and restraint.

I suggest you live life by these three words—give, save, and spend—and experience freedom from debt. When you do, you can stop letting money be the boss that tells you what you will be doing with your time. Instead, as you follow God's principles, you will watch Him restore the financial situation in your home.

— ❖❖❖❖ —

Live life by these three words—give, save, and spend—and experience freedom from debt.

— ❖❖❖❖ —

11

❖❖❖❖❖❖

ROMANCE

I WANT YOU TO REMEMBER the first time you kissed your spouse. It shouldn't be hard. Most of us can recall that moment of anticipation, the buildup of hormones and emotions, and the culmination of coming together. In fact, scientists have researched the effects of kissing, along with the transmission of sensory data that takes place, and concluded that kissing is one of the most profound things a person can do. The impact of a kiss, when all things line up right, can leave an even more powerful sensory imprint on our brains than something as major as the first time a person ever had sex.

"Whether it's magic or a disaster," writes Sheril Kirshenbaum, author of *The Science of Kissing*, "there is one thing that a first kiss is very likely to be: unforgettable."[1]

Kirshenbaum goes on to say,

Psychologist John Bohannon of Butler University and his research team surveyed 500 people to compare their recollections of a variety of significant life experiences—such as a first kiss and the loss of virginity—to find out what made the most dramatic impression. *A first kiss trumped everything*: It was the most vivid memory in the minds of those being surveyed. In fact, when asked about specifics, Bohannon reported that most people could recall up to 90 percent of the details of the moment—where they were, who made the first move—no matter how long ago the exchange took place.[2]

There is a biological reason for this that God, in His infinite wisdom, has created within us. Over the centuries, we have only had the ability to experience romantic love rather than to study it. Anthropologists have discovered evidence of the existence of romantic love in 170 different societies, yet they have never found a society in which it didn't exist.[3] Romance has been around from as far back as we can determine, and it even shows up as the major emphasis in an entire book of the Bible, the Song of Solomon.

Romance is such a powerful part of who we are because God has created us in such a way that we attach to our romantic partner based not only on our thoughts, interactions, and conversations with each other but on our senses.

——— ❖❖❖❖❖ ———

Romance is a powerful part of who we are.

——— ❖❖❖❖❖ ———

Yet as scientific research has shown us, the parts of our brains that are aroused through romance aren't necessarily the same parts aroused through sex. Romance that evokes emotions of love often involves a complex transference of biological signals, including smell, touch, and taste. That's why kissing is critical to long-term attachment. As we kiss, God has designed our blood vessels to dilate, thus providing our brains with more oxygen.

Scientists have also observed that our pupils dilate when we kiss. An open-mouthed kiss allows nearly ten thousand taste buds on our tongues to transmit additional information to our brains, which then respond by producing certain hormones designed to strengthen attachment between two people.[4]

Sheril Kirshenbaum writes that

kissing also promotes the "love hormone," oxytocin, which works to maintain a special connection between two people; kissing can keep love alive when a relationship has survived decades, long after novelty has waned. In other words, kissing influences the uptake of hormones and neurotransmitters beyond our conscious control, and these signals play a huge part in how we feel about each other.

A bad kiss, alternatively, can lead to chemical chaos. An uncomfortable environment or a poor match can stimulate the "stress hormone" cortisol, discouraging both partners from continuing.[5]

Most married couples can attest that it's possible to have sexual relations without romance, but it's rare to have romance without sex. Of course, there are times when one spouse may not be able to have sex due to age or illness, but if the romance is there and both are able, sex is the natural culmination of shared romantic affection.

Some of this is because when romantic ties are stimulated in our bodies and brains, our bodies respond by producing chemicals

Sex without a foundation of romance will not restore a relationship.

that create a desire for deeper connection and bonds, more so than by sex. This explains why counselors who encourage struggling couples to increase their sexual activity are ineffective. They aren't focusing on the core components of love. After four decades of counseling hundreds and hundreds of struggling couples, I've heard more often than not that it's possible to have sex when you are not in love. Sex doesn't create love; it's intended as the culmination of love.

Thus, couples who are struggling in their relationships need to focus on rekindling both their connection and their romance—whether that's through kind words, actions, listening, or intimate kissing and nonsexual touch— before looking to regain the sexual chemistry they may have once shared.

Sex without a foundation of romance will not restore a relationship. We all know that sexual intimacy involves much more than two bodies enjoying physical contact with each other and exchanging a pleasurable experience. If that were all that was necessary for intimate bonding to happen between two people, then prostitutes would have the most emotionally, physically, and spiritually intimate relationships in the world.

Yada, Yada, Yada

I'll never forget an experience I had a few years ago. I had been preparing to preach a sermon series on knowing God intimately when I stumbled upon one of the most revealing principles on sexuality I'd ever encountered. It came under the umbrella of what it means to "know" God. But as I looked at the original Hebrew language, I discovered that Scripture had couched this truth of spiritual intimacy with God in the midst of something that matters deeply to all of us: human intimacy with each other; in particular, with our spouses.

I learned in seminary, many years back, that whenever you approach the study of Scripture, and, in particular, when you are seeking to discover the meaning of a specific phrase, word, or principle, it is best to use the hermeneutical law of first mention. The concept of origination is an important tool in the Bible. According to this study practice, the original meaning tied to a word or principle is to stand contiguous throughout future uses of the same word or principle unless the biblical text itself instructs you to change it at a later point. With that in mind, the first mention of sexual intimacy occurs in Genesis 4:1: "Now the man *had relations* with his wife Eve, and she conceived and gave birth."

Were we to look at the original language, we would discover that the word translated "had relations" in English is the Hebrew word *yada*.[6] Interestingly, it is the identical word used earlier when the eyes of Adam and Eve were opened, and they "knew" they were naked. It's also the same word used in Genesis 3:22: "Then the LORD God said, 'Behold, the man has become like one of Us, *knowing* good and evil.'"

Although this word *yada* in Genesis 4:1 speaks of something we would call sex or physical intimacy today, the word itself doesn't refer to body parts or physical activity. In more than one thousand occurrences of the word in the Old Testament, it has these meanings:

- to cause to know
- to reveal oneself
- to be made known, be revealed
- to make oneself known
- to know

When the word *yada* is used with a relational connection, whether that connection is human to human or human to God, it reveals a depth of plummeting into the reality of another person in order to know deeply and be deeply known. So intimate is this term when used as the "first mention" to introduce sexual relations in Scripture that when applied to God, it is included in some of the most personal interactions we can have with Him:

> I will give you the treasures of darkness
> And hidden wealth of secret places,
> So that you may *know* [*yada*] that it is I,
> The LORD, the God of Israel, who calls you by your name. (Isaiah 45:3)

> The secret of the LORD is for those who fear Him,
> And He will make them *know* [*yada*] His covenant. (Psalm 25:14)

> "You are My witnesses," declares the LORD,
> "And My servant whom I have chosen,
> So that you may *know* [*yada*] and believe Me." (Isaiah 43:10)

In these passages we read about "treasures of darkness," being "chosen," the Lord's "secret," and "secret places." These words refer to our relationship with God, but we also use them with one another in a close, marital tie. One thing is true about secrets: You either have to be in close proximity to whisper them, or at a minimum, you have to be close in trust to share them. God says we are close to Him in that way when we *yada* (*know*) Him.

True sexual intimacy, which includes the romantic ties of knowing and being known, shares much more than moments of passion. It is experienced because two people share secrets, their biology,

> *True sexual intimacy, which includes the romantic ties of knowing and being known, shares much more than moments of passion.*

pheromones, fears, failures, hopes, dreams, trust, and even more. Through a romantic bond with each other, couples find the most authentic form of love possible. In fact, the very secret nature of what they share becomes its own treasure. After all, what makes a secret a secret? It is a secret because no one else shares in it.

The same is true in sex and romance. When either married individual shares that aspect of intimacy with someone outside of the marriage covenant, he or she has broken the sacredness of the secret treasure once shared with his or her spouse. When that happens, this bond of *yada* morphs from what God intended it to be into what Satan sought to corrupt it into, which is known in Scripture as *porneuō*[7] or *shakab*.[8]

These biblical terms refer to the exact same act of sexuality as *yada*, but they remove the sacred nature of the act and replace it with the shallowness of commonality. In doing so, the individuals involved have removed one of the main purposes and intentions of sexuality: the exclusive bonding (emotionally, spiritually, chemically) that allows for knowing and being known.

When sex becomes nothing more than an activity to perform for its own end, it brings with it heartbreak, jealousy, regret, and emotional, physical, and spiritual consequences. This is true even in marriages, as we see the term *shakab* used for sexual relations between Jacob and Leah, the wife he did not love. If you read about Jacob and Leah's marriage in Genesis 29, you will discover it was rife with pain, loss, regret, and conflict. Here are some other instances in Scripture where the term *shakab* is used instead of *yada*:

- David being sexually intimate with Bathsheba (2 Samuel 11)
- Shechem defiling Dinah (Genesis 34)
- Reuben having sexual relations with Bilhah, his father's concubine (Genesis 35:22)
- Amnon raping Tamar (2 Samuel 13)
- Lot's daughters having sex with their father (Genesis 19:30–38)

Sex in and of itself is not intimacy that leads to a deeper relational tie. Married couples can have sex during their entire marriage and yet never experience *yada*. This is because *yada* involves much more than an action. It includes the elements of romantic attachment, desire, cultivation, and commitment regarding another person, which lead to a depth of knowing in a marriage. This is the kind of intimacy that arouses feelings of satisfaction, contentment, happiness, and joy with each other on an ongoing basis.

It has often been said that sex doesn't begin in the bedroom; it begins in the kitchen. But actually, sex doesn't begin in the bedroom or the kitchen; it begins in the brain. Scientists have been studying what is often called the unique "odor-prints" each of us has, which are similar to a fingerprint. Odorprints are made up of pheromones and other odors that can trigger attraction between certain people.[9] These pheromones and other odors may not only be used during the dating cycle to help us determine the best potential mate for us, but they can also be used during marriage to maintain attraction and arousal between partners. In fact, in one study, postmenopausal, married women who no longer produced their own pheromones were given synthetically made pheromones similar to those of younger women. In this double-blind, placebo-controlled study, the women given the pheromones showed a dramatic increase not only in sexual activity with their husbands but also in romantic activities such as cuddling and intentional dates.[10]

Sex doesn't begin in the bedroom or the kitchen; it begins in the brain.

Beyond smell, the acts of viewing, hearing, touch, arousal, and orgasm involve a highly complex mixture of chemicals and chemical responses as well, each designed to regulate an intended connection by our Creator. In fact, these chemicals—oxytocin, in particular—strengthen our willingness to trust each other as spouses, which is one reason many believe that "pillow talk" after sex, or during breaks while having sex, is such an intimate experience. During those times we are chemically wired to let down our guard and trust more deeply than at any other time. This relational sharing then leads to a greater knowing (*yada*), which deepens the relationship overall.[11]

God uses the understanding and experience of intimacy in our marriage relationships to give us clues to the unique intimacy within the Trinity, and it also serves as a down payment on the intimacy His children will experience with the Lord in eternity. Jesus made it clear, in his High Priestly Prayer, that He wanted the unity and oneness of His followers to share in the joyful experience of intimacy that He Himself shared with His Father (John 17:5, 13, 21). Since marriage is the highest form of oneness God created on earth, it stands to reason that it should be the primary context, on a human level, for tapping into the intimacy of the Godhead. It also explains why marriage will no longer be needed in heaven, since we will have the full and direct experience of intimacy with God (Matthew 22:30).

Watching Over Your Marriage with All Diligence

Within marriage, the chemical bonds of romance that God has given us serve a greater purpose of creating ties of commitment, attraction, and protection. Yet unfortunately when these experiences occur outside the boundaries of marriage (such as in a romantic and/or physical affair), they not only damage the marital attachment, thus requiring the married couple to rebuild what they lost if they are to restore relational harmony, but they also create chemical bonds that have been shown to leave lasting scars, cravings, and even symptoms of withdrawal for months or even years when ultimately broken. Extramarital relations (whether physical or emotionally romantic) do far more damage than breaking trust through betrayal in a marriage; they literally transfer the marital chemical bond with one partner to someone else. Measurable scientific data has shown that the withdrawal from a temporary love interest is as severe as the withdrawal from any drug, if not more severe.[12]

> ❖❖❖❖❖
>
> *Extramarital relations (whether physical or emotionally romantic) do far more damage than breaking trust through betrayal in a marriage.*
>
> ❖❖❖❖❖

We're now learning this through science, but God has known that for all time. He has even told us something very similar in His Word. When the apostle Paul used the word *kollaō*[13] when speaking about a man having relations with a prostitute, it's no wonder that he chose a word that literally means "to glue together, cement." He wrote, "Do you not know that the one who *joins* himself to a prostitute is one body with her?" (1 Corinthians 6:16). Sexual and romantic activities both release chemicals designed to bond, and these brain-imprinting hormones literally glue or cement individuals together.

When an illicit relationship is stopped, strong physiological reactions occur in the brain very similar to what happens when the use of drugs, alcohol, or other addictive substances is stopped. Anytime a person stops an addictive behavior without addressing it spiritually through the steps of acknowledgment, repentance, forgiveness, healing, empowerment, and freedom, that person has a higher chance of returning to that behavior, or a similar behavior, at a later time.

Failure to address and heal spiritually from marital infidelity (whether romantic or sexual) can be compared to taking away an alcoholic's favorite brand of beer and then sending him back into a bar with countless other brands to choose from. Could he stop drinking his favorite brand of beer? Yes. But would he have the emotional, physical, and spiritual tools necessary to turn down the opportunity to try another brand on another day? Probably not.

That is why Scripture teaches us to "watch over your heart with all diligence, for from it flow the springs of life" (Proverbs 4:23). It's far easier to watch over your heart and body with all diligence than to heal your heart, as well as the heart of the spouse you have hurt and betrayed. Romantic and/or physical connection with someone outside of marriage defiles the bond of the covenant. In fact, Jesus goes so far as to tell us that a man has committed adultery

It's far easier to watch over your heart and body with all diligence than to heal your heart, as well as the heart of the spouse you have hurt and betrayed.

with a woman even if he looks on her with lust (Matthew 5:28). Adultery is deeper than the physical act because it is rooted in a spiritual source. While the law focused on the action (Exodus 20:14), Jesus focused on the heart.

When a man looks at a woman intentionally—I don't mean a passing glance to appreciate or admire the God-given beauty of a woman, which is not a sin—but when a man elongates the glance or takes it further in his mind, that is lust. Lust in any form, including pornography, is immorality. As Peter wrote, "With eyes full of adultery, [these men] never stop sinning; they seduce the unstable" (2 Peter 2:14, NIV).

Giving to Each Other

So how do we protect our hearts and bodies with all diligence in regard to romance in our marriages? One way is outlined for us in 1 Corinthians 7:3–4:

> The husband must fulfill his duty to his wife, and likewise also the wife to her husband. The wife does not have authority over her own body, but the husband does; and likewise also the husband does not have authority over his own body, but the wife does.

Paul used the word *duty* in reference to physical intimacy, which gives us a unique way of viewing this sacred act. A duty is specifically designed to be other generated, to fulfill something that someone else needs. In addition, Paul specifically reminded his readers that neither the wife nor the husband has authority over their own bodies. Both of them belong to each other. Both spouses need sexual and romantic experiences in their marriage, and one spouse may need to be intimate at a time when the other doesn't necessarily feel like it. That's why Paul admonished both spouses to fulfill their duty.

> *One of the greatest obstacles to developing true physical intimacy in a marriage is a failure to correctly comprehend the needs of the other person.*

Many men have said to me in counseling, "I would love to fulfill my duty to my wife, but she won't let me."

My response to them is always the same: "That could be because what you are offering to fulfill, she doesn't need."

One of the greatest obstacles to developing true physical intimacy in a marriage is a failure to correctly comprehend the needs of the other person and then meet those needs first. Duty goes beyond physical intimacy.

What a woman needs starts in the morning and not at night; it starts with her emotions and not her body. Some husbands fail to grasp what their wives truly need, and then when they show up at 10:00 PM ready to meet *her* needs, they receive a cold shoulder rather than a warm embrace. Husbands, if the only time your wife knows she can count on you to be with her is when you want physical relations with her, then you are not meeting her emotional and relational needs. That is why 1 Peter 3:7 tells us as husbands to understand our wives. Most of our wives were attracted to us at least in part because of what we did during the dating period. One thing we did was talk in a way that caused them to respond positively.

Another thing a lot of men were good at when they were dating their future wives was making them feel special and planning little surprises. A guy would open the car door and wait until his date got in, and then close it softly behind her. Now she's lucky to get into the car before he drives off. When she was about to go through a door, the guy would open it for her. Now the door hits her as he walks through ahead of her.

Husbands, your wives desired to marry you not because you stripped down and talked about your manly attributes. They desired to marry you because you met their emotional, relational, and even romantic needs. Those needs don't change after you say "I do."

In counseling, wives will often share that their need for affection and a sense of security, communication, and being cared for and esteemed is not being met. As the romance leaves a relationship, the passion for sex often dwindles as well. When couples tell me they have a sexual problem, that is rarely true. In most cases, what they have is an intimacy problem, a relational problem. Because of this, they cannot get the physical part of their marriage working.

But wives, I also want to address you, because Paul admonished you to meet your husbands' needs as well. A wife can't simply look to her own wants in a marriage without caring for what is important to her husband. Your husband will often desire regular physical intimacy, but there are other things that can help meet his needs as well. One is your appearance and grooming, which wives often overlook once a busy schedule or kids enter into the equation. Try to remember how you spent so much time preparing yourself for your husband when you were dating, and strive to keep yourself as attractive to him as you did before you said "I do."

Wives, your husbands cannot date you, care for you, compliment you, serve you, and make sure your needs are met only to have you deny theirs. To receive your husband's love and affection without reciprocating in ways that are meaningful to him will ultimately lead to a lack of intimacy as well. When a husband is fulfilling his duty to his wife, the wife responds to his lead by relinquishing her body to the touch, care, caress, and love of her husband. Likewise, as the husband responds to her response to him, he also relinquishes his body to her. The picture in these verses Paul penned is of two people belonging totally to each other. Through the mystery of sex, married couples discover an intimate level of giving themselves through a unique vulnerability and mutual yielding.

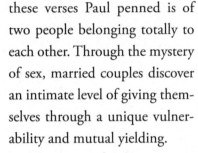

Through the mystery of sex, married couples discover an intimate level of giving themselves through a unique vulnerability and mutual yielding.

The Song of Solomon contains the Bible's most unblushing description of sexual intimacy in marriage. Chapter 4 describes the buildup to intimacy in great detail, and the beauty of it is that you see the self-giving between Solomon and his wife, the mutual yielding of their bodies.

The intimacy begins with Solomon's compliments and words of admiration and appreciation for his bride, not with the physical act of sex. But when the moment of sexual intimacy occurs, God Himself invites the lovers to enjoy each other (Song of Solomon 5:1) in an act He has given married couples as one of the most deeply rewarding and mutually familiar ways of engaging each other.

Honoring Your Intimacy

A lot of attention is paid to the area of sexuality in a marriage because sexual intimacy is important to the ongoing health and vitality of the relationship. But another area is often overlooked, and I want to touch on it briefly as we close out this chapter on romance. This often-overlooked area is willingly honoring your ongoing intimacy with your spouse.

What do I mean by honoring your intimacy? I mean respecting and cherishing the special depth of communication, visual and physical freedom, and interchange that happens in a marriage relationship.

Husbands and wives will often open up with each other about areas in their lives that they may not feel free to discuss with others, including their fears, ambitions, hidden thoughts, or even fantasies. These intimate exchanges of your souls with each other, which can often occur as pillow talk before or after sex, should be protected and esteemed. Don't use times of intimate sharing to correct, belittle, or interrogate your spouse. Not only that, but strive to cherish these secretly shared conversations by leaving them in the protective privacies where you shared them. Bringing them up again at the kitchen table or in the more common activities of life can have a way of dampening the special moments you enjoyed. Protect each other's hearts, and you will be rewarded with deeper intimacy of both body and mind.

The picture in these verses Paul penned is of two people belonging totally to each other.

Honoring your spouse in the area of intimacy also includes your personal presentation and interaction. Far too often I've seen once very attractive husbands and wives completely let themselves go after getting married. For whatever reason, they paid great attention not only to their looks but also to how they presented themselves before the wedding, but very little after. Or as is often the case in counseling, spouses will comment that the only time they get to see their mates as they used to be is on special occasions or dates. The rest of the time, wives are fine with wearing sweatpants, T-shirts, and no makeup, and husbands are fine being sloppy and ungroomed.

The two of you are a gift to each other every day. Celebrate that gift. What you share together is precious and can never be shared at that level with anyone else. That doesn't mean you need to dress to the nines all the time, but why not honor your spouse by paying special attention to how you appear in his or her eyes? Why not want your spouse to continue seeing you and treasuring you as the light of his or her eyes?

When you walk into the room, do you still catch his attention? Or does he have to wait for a date to say, "Wow!" Husbands, can she hear the leftovers of your lunch being burped up from the next room, or do you honor her by letting her live as a lady in the presence of a gentleman?

Honoring your intimacy also means keeping your language with each other sacred. I've heard spouses talk to each other or demand something from each other when they didn't think someone else was nearby or listening, and it made me cringe. The tone was abrupt, and the word choices were direct and self-serving. If it made me cringe, how do you think it made the spouse feel? Yet this seems to happen all too often in marriages.

Or often husbands and wives will use each other not as a sounding board but as a venting machine. They lower the honor of their intimacy in such a way that one or both of them feel free to complain about life, work, each other, friends, or anything else. Sharing stressful situations with your spouse is important and healthy in giving and finding support. But allowing your conversations to deteriorate to such a degree that your spouse has to carry your personal load and burdens verbally each and every day will diminish the sacredness of your verbal space.

Honoring your intimacy also means keeping your language with each other sacred.

Romance includes bringing joy to each other in a variety of ways, and one way to always do that is by keeping your tone, your words, and your touch imbued with respect and allure. Don't save the kind words or pet names just for the bedroom or on the dates, while turning your relationship into a place for constant unloading of your day's weight. Marriage was designed as a way of bringing out the best in both of you so that you can jointly fulfill God's purposes in your lives. Enjoy this gift He has given you. Honor it. Cherish it. And keep the romance alive.

12

REBUILDING

MOST OF US HAVE SEEN implosions on television where buildings are brought down. This typically happens when an old, dilapidated building is taking up valuable space that could be used for something else. Dynamite is strategically placed in the building to implode it, thus lowering it from whatever height it is into a pile of rubble.

No matter how long it took construction crews to erect the building—weeks, months, or even years—it only requires a few seconds to destroy it. All because an implosion has occurred.

Unfortunately, today many marriages are imploding from explosive outbursts or harmful words. With our tongues, we have the capacity to quickly destroy each other's hope and emotional health, bringing down what may have taken years to build up in our relationships.

> *With our tongues, we have the capacity to quickly destroy each other's hope and emotional health, bringing down what may have taken years to build up in our relationships.*

Scripture points us in the opposite direction with regard to how we are to use our words with each other. Rather than tearing one another down, the Bible instructs us to intentionally build up, develop, and edify each other through what we say. We read in several places,

So then we pursue the things which make for peace and the *building up* of one another. (Romans 14:19)

Let all things be done for *edification.* (1 Corinthians 14:26)

Speaking the truth in love, we are to grow up in all aspects into Him who is the head, even Christ, from whom the whole body, being fitted and held together by what every joint supplies, according to the proper working of each individual part, causes the growth of the body for the *building up* of itself in love. (Ephesians 4:15–16)

Encourage one another and *build up* one another, just as you also are doing. (1 Thessalonians 5:11)

Too many couples are known for tearing each other down rather than building each other up. Perhaps it's a sly remark in public or withholding a kind word when out with friends. Maybe it's done in private, behind closed doors. Whatever the case, our words can either wound or infuse life. They are powerful. A healthy marriage is one where both partners treat with care this critical area of what they say to each other.

The Power of Your Words

The Bible is clear that when it comes to relating to one another, we are to be construction workers who are building something, not demolition crews tearing things down. Of all of the places on the planet, your marriage should be that one place where you are encouraged, reminded of your strengths, and given the motivation you need to live out those strengths well. When was the last time you complimented your spouse, with no ulterior motive attached? If you were asked to do so, could you accurately identify your spouse's top skills, strengths, and character qualities? Does your spouse truly know the things about himself or herself that attract you?

A powerful prayer to include in your time with the Lord might go something like this:

Dear Father, help me to always use my words to build up my mate so that he/she can fully live out the destiny You have chosen for him/her. Help me to focus on his/her strengths and overlook, or lovingly correct, the weak areas so that what I have to say produces life and not death.

It's a simple prayer but one I encourage you to add to your arsenal as a prayer warrior. Far too often, couples focus on "helping" each other grow by pointing out weaknesses, even in their prayers. How about rather than pointing out your mate's mistakes to the Lord in prayer (He already knows them anyway), you take the time to thank God for your mate's good qualities. Make this a habit, and soon you'll experience a shift in how you view and talk to your spouse.

Your marriage should be that one place where you are encouraged, reminded of your strengths, and given the motivation you need to live out those strengths well.

Building each other up begins with a mind-set that values the importance of edification in words. Ephesians 4:29 says, "Let no unwholesome word proceed from your mouth, but only such a word as is good for edification according to the need of the moment, so that it will give grace to those who hear." In this passage, edification is tied directly to communication.

Despite our best attempts at diminishing the perceived impact of communication, words matter. Maybe you've heard the saying "Sticks and stones may break my bones, but words will never hurt me." I don't know who came up with that, or even why, because that statement couldn't be further from the truth. Entire marriages have been ruined by things that were said, or by things that were repeated over a period of time. Lives have been wrecked by words. The reality is that words do matter, and what you hear affects how you think and feel, and ultimately how you act.

If a judge were to pronounce you guilty or innocent in a trial, those two words would matter greatly simply because they impact your freedom. If a doctor were to walk into the treatment room and say either "Benign" or "Malignant," trust me, those words would matter because they affect the nature of your well-being. Words can literally control your emotional health, or lack thereof, if you let them, which most of us do.

———— ✤✤✤✤✤ ————

What you say, how you say it, and even when you say it affects whether you are building someone up or tearing someone down.

———— ✤✤✤✤✤ ————

What you say, how you say it, and even when you say it affects whether you are building someone up or tearing someone down. Your mouth reveals your heart and simultaneously affects someone else's, for good or for bad.

Wisdom in Words

In your marriage, the goal of edification through communication is to build each other up. When your spouse has to face criticism at work, in the community, with extended-family members, or even from your children, your marriage should be that one safe haven where he or she can be sure of receiving encouragement and love. That doesn't mean you never point out anything that might need to be improved, but you speak "the truth in love" (Ephesians 4:15), making love and truth the two goalposts through which your words must pass.

The bitterness in which so many marriages rot today reminds me of a story once told of Lady Astor and Winston Churchill. They served in the British Parliament together and openly hated each other. One day Lady Astor said to Winston Churchill, "If you were my husband, I'd poison your tea."

To which Winston Churchill replied, "Madam, if you were my wife, I'd drink it."

We chuckle at the extremism of those sentiments, but you would be amazed at the things husbands and wives say to each other. Perhaps you've even done it yourself, or had it said to you. Having counseled married couples for nearly four decades now, I've heard it all. And the tongue, by far, is one of the most powerful tools—for good or for bad. As we saw earlier in Ephesians 4:29, we are to speak in such a way that we "give grace" to the one who hears our words. One way to view communicating with our spouses is as a ministry of grace, which is the purpose after all. Grace means favor—quite literally unmerited favor.

It shouldn't matter whether your spouse deserves to have you say nice things. It shouldn't matter if he or she has earned your approval. According to God's Word, you are to use your words and your tone to minister grace in your marriage. Aren't you glad that God doesn't wait until you deserve His grace to give it to you? Neither should you hold your spouse hostage to a certain standard to minister grace to him or her in what you say.

Seasoned with Salt

How you say what you say is often just as important as *what* you say. It's like the husband who was looking after his wife's elderly mother as well as the dog, which the wife loved very much. His wife needed to run out and do some errands. When she came back a few hours later, she asked, "Where's the dog?"

Her husband replied, "The dog is dead."

"What?" she shrieked. "I can't believe you just blurted that out to me like that! Instead of just saying, 'The dog is dead,' why didn't you at least try to soften the blow some? You could have said, 'The dog was on the roof, slipped, and didn't make it.'"

> How *you say what you say is often just as important as* what *you say.*

Some time went by, and the wife noticed she hadn't seen her mother, who was living with them at the time. So she asked her husband, "Where's my mother?"

The husband thought about what she had said about the dog, so he replied, "Well, your mom was on the roof . . ."

Are you direct in your speech with your spouse? Is there room for you to soften what you say? Have you lost the art of being polite when it comes to how you talk to your mate? Too many marriages today are punctuated with harsh talk. If you wouldn't talk to your coworkers, your boss, or even a stranger at the grocery store that way, why do you think it is loving, kind, and relationally effective to talk to your spouse that way?

Our Lord instructs us in Colossians 4:6 to "let your speech always be with grace, as though seasoned with salt, so that you will know how you should respond to each person." In other words, put some flavor on your words so that you make them as tasty as possible and remove the option for decay. That's what salt does; it adds flavor and inhibits decay. If you are interested in spicing up your marriage, add salt to what you say. If you are interested in preserving your marriage, add salt to what you say. Intentionally choose both tone and language that edify the other person, and you will be amazed at what that does to improve your relationship. When speaking to your spouse, be sure to flavor your communication so that what you say is not only edible but also digestible.

If we as couples would begin to adopt the attitude and approach of seeking to minister to each other with our words with the goal of building each other up, we would get less "reaction" from each other and less conflict with each other. We would also cut down on the amount of competition, anger, regret, and pain that we experience in our marriages. Wouldn't it be nice to have a marriage punctuated by grace and peace rather than jabs and pain? It's possible if you will just commit to edifying each other.

Taming the Tongue

The book of James is a small book that packs a big punch. It has a lot to say about our words. In chapter 3, James introduced a comprehensive analogy for the tongue:

> Look at the ships also, though they are so great and are driven by strong winds, are still directed by a very small rudder wherever the inclination of the pilot desires. So also the tongue is a small part of the body, and yet it boasts of great things.
>
> See how great a forest is set aflame by such a small fire! And the tongue is a fire, the very world of iniquity; the tongue is set among our members as that which defiles the entire body, and sets on fire the course of our life, and is set on fire by hell. For every species of beasts and birds, of reptiles and creatures of the sea, is tamed and has been

tamed by the human race. But no one can tame the tongue; it is a restless evil and full of deadly poison. With it we bless our Lord and Father, and with it we curse men, who have been made in the likeness of God; from the same mouth come both blessing and cursing. My brethren, these things ought not to be this way. Does a fountain send out from the same opening both fresh and bitter water? Can a fig tree, my brethren, produce olives, or a vine produce figs? Nor can salt water produce fresh. (verses 4–12)

Friend, if God is in charge of your mouth, you shouldn't give double messages. We shouldn't hear you praising God and cursing others. You shouldn't speak one way in church in front of the members of the family of God and another way in the presence of your own family. The tongue is a powerful tool, as James mentioned, like a rudder that can direct a massive ship. Your tongue, and what you say, has the ability to steer your marriage toward mutual satisfaction and benefit or mutual despair and harm. Choose your words carefully, because within them is housed both life and death.

❖❖❖❖

Choose your words carefully, because within them is housed both life and death.

❖❖❖❖

You not only affect your marriage with what you say, but you also affect your relationship with God. Let's take a more expanded look at Ephesians 4:29–32, which I touched on earlier. In this passage we discover how what we say to one another actually impacts the level of our own personal intimacy with God, which in turn affects our access to His abundance, power, grace, and forgiveness, which we so desperately need:

Let no unwholesome word proceed from your mouth. . . . Do not grieve the Holy Spirit of God, by whom you were sealed for the day of redemption. Let all bitterness and wrath and anger and clamor and slander be put away from you, along with all malice. Be kind to one another, tender-hearted, forgiving each other, just as God in Christ also has forgiven you.

Most of us don't realize that the unkind words we say to our spouses grieve the Holy Spirit of God. But they do. I'm sure that if we were more aware of that fact, we would be more careful with our words. The Holy Spirit is saddened by our speech, because speech is a spiritual issue, not just a conversation piece. What you say and how you say it ought not to depend on the perfection or performance of your mate. It ought to be entirely dependent upon God's tenderness, kindness, grace, and forgiveness toward you. Use God's treatment of you as your standard for how you are to treat your spouse.

Now I have an idea of what you might be thinking right now. *But, Tony, you don't know what my spouse did to me. You don't know how my spouse hurt me, dismissed me, yelled at me . . . or all of the above.* And you are right. I don't know, but God does. And He is the one who gave us our instructions regarding our tongues. Despite anything and everything that may have been said or done to you, God still says to mind your words. I've taken the liberty to recast the following passage in marital terms, with substituted words italicized:

> Do not speak against *your spouse*. . . . He who speaks against *his or her spouse*, . . . speaks against the law and judges the law; but if you judge the law, you are not a doer of the law but a judge of it. There is only one Lawgiver and Judge, the One who is able to save and to destroy; but who are you who judge *your spouse*? (James 4:11–12)

If that isn't straightforward enough, God punctuates His point in chapter 5, and again, I've cast it in marital terms. "Do not complain, brethren, against *your spouse*, so that you yourselves may not be judged; behold, the Judge is standing right at the door" (verse 9).

I didn't say it; God did. Do not even complain. To complain against someone presumes that there is something about which to complain. Anyone who is married has legitimate things to complain about regarding his or her spouse simply because we married human beings who came complete with sinful natures, just like we did. Yes, you've been hurt by your spouse. Yes, you may have been neglected, overlooked, or harshly spoken to. But God is clear: Do not complain. Leave room for Him to handle your spouse by leaving your complaints in His hands.

When you hold your tongue and use it instead in obedience to God to edify your spouse rather than complain, you open the door for God's hand to redeem, correct, challenge, and restore your mate to a right relationship with you. Too many times, married couples will stay the hand of God by taking things into their own hands, primarily with their mouths.

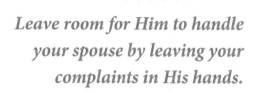

Leave room for Him to handle your spouse by leaving your complaints in His hands.

Earlier in James 5:8, we read, "You too, be patient and stand firm, because the Lord's coming is near" (NIV). He is closer and His coming to deliver us is sooner than we might think. But while you wait on God to intervene, don't allow your frustration with your spouse to cause you to take it out on him or her. Because if you do, then instead of the Lord coming to be near you as it says in verse 8 of James 5, you'll get verse 9, the Lord coming to judge you: "Don't grumble against each other, brothers, or you will be judged" (NIV).

In verse 8, God is coming through for you. In verse 9, He's coming to judge you. And the only difference between verses 8 and 9 is your mouth. The difference between God coming through for you or coming to judge you in your marriage is what you say. In other words, watch your mouth, because your mouth may be blocking your blessing. Your tongue may be blocking your deliverance. God may be right at the door ready to restore, but then He hears what you say to your spouse, and He shuts it.

It was the Israelites' mouths that kept them from entering the Promised Land. Every time they faced a challenge, they complained. They were fussing about not having enough water, not having enough food, wondering why they couldn't just go back to Egypt . . . and more! So for forty years, the Lord let the Israelites wander in their misery rather than enjoy the blessings of His abundant provision and promises, because they talked too much about the wrong things.

It's like the cowboy who was driving down the highway in his truck with his dog beside him and pulling his horse in a trailer. When he hit a corner too hard, they all flipped. A policeman arrived at the scene shortly after the accident happened. He walked up to the horse and saw that he wasn't going to make it, so he took out his gun and shot the horse to relieve him of his pain. Then he walked over to the dog and saw that he was near death and in agony, so he relieved him as well. After that he walked over to the cowboy and asked how he felt. Seeing the smoke still coming from the gun, the cowboy quickly said, "I ain't never felt better!"

All kidding aside, your words can save your life. Not only that, they can save your marriage. Choose to speak blessing into your home and your spouse on a daily basis. Rather than complaining, text words that edify your spouse, and see what happens. You'll be amazed. No one wants to be stuck in a miserable marriage, but that misery can change to blessing if you will commit to intentionally choosing what you say based on God's principles. Do this, and the entire atmosphere of your home will improve.

> ❖❖❖❖❖
>
> *Choose to speak blessing into your home and your spouse on a daily basis.*
>
> ❖❖❖❖❖

Let David's prayer be your own daily prayer for your marriage: "Let the words of my mouth and the meditation of my heart be acceptable in Your sight, O LORD, my rock and my Redeemer" (Psalm 19:14). Pray that verse each morning and abide by it, and you will see life restored in your marriage.

Mouth-to-mouth resuscitation gives life. So does mouth-to-mouth maturity in what we choose to say and not say.

13

❖❖❖❖❖❖

RETURN

A MARRIED WOMAN ONCE SAID, "I was looking for the ideal, but instead it became an ordeal, and now I want a new deal."

A man put it this way: "Marriage has become like a three-ring circus: engagement ring, wedding ring, and suffering."

It is possible to live in the same house with someone and not enjoy much of a home. This occurs when love deteriorates into duty, when passion morphs into programs, and when communication becomes sticky notes, grunts, or text messages.

It's like the husband and wife who stopped speaking to each other for an inordinate amount of time due to some conflict they'd

❖❖❖❖❖

It's possible to live in the same house with someone and not enjoy much of a home.

❖❖❖❖❖

had. Not wanting to be late for his flight the next morning, the husband wrote a note and put it on the wife's side of the bed the night before. The note read, "Wake me up at five o'clock so that I can catch my flight."

When the husband woke up, he realized it was seven thirty, and he had missed his flight. Furious that his wife didn't wake him up, he looked to her side of the bed. She was gone, but in her place was a note that read, "It's five o'clock."

You also know your marriage relationship is heading south when compliments become criticisms. One man was so frustrated with his wife that he said, "I can't believe God made someone so beautiful and simultaneously so stupid."

To which she replied, "Well, you're right. God made me beautiful so you would love me, but he made me stupid so I would love you."

Now that level of sarcasm sounds a bit harsh, but based on the countless counseling sessions I've conducted with married couples, it isn't unusual. Relationship breakdowns come in all shapes and sizes and affect all manner of ways in which spouses relate to each other.

This is sometimes not too dissimilar to the breakdowns we experience in our relationship with God. Believers can go days or even weeks without having any meaningful communication with the Lord. Or the communication we do have may be entirely one-sided. God addressed the heart of our relationship with Him in the book of Revelation, and while this doesn't deal specifically with marriage, the principles He gives us for how we relate to Him can cross over and apply in a number of ways to how married couples relate to each other. Exploring the heart of the matter with God can help us better understand the heart of the matter with our spouses.

The passage I want to focus on is part of a letter that was written to seven churches, wherein our Lord described how He felt about His relationship with each of them. The first church He addressed was the church of Ephesus, which could be considered the modern day New York City of Asia Minor. Ephesus was the place to be where things were happening in commerce, international trade, and even societal gatherings. Ephesus housed the cultural expression of that time, along with the religious activity, with the Temple of Diana as the centerpiece for much of life. Ephesus held potential and promise in most every way. Life flowed through her streets.

A church had been birthed in Ephesus through the work and ministry of the apostle Paul, and in the beginning, the people in the church were on fire for God (Acts 19). They had brought out their trinkets, magic books, and anything else associated with their old way of life and literally set it all ablaze out of devotion to God. Their relationship with the Lord was one of passion, zeal, and connection.

Many relationships are like this when couples first get married. Personal sacrifice doesn't feel like sacrifice. Devotion comes naturally. Yet over time, as we will see in Revelation, that passion somehow morphs into performance as something in the relationship fizzles.

The letter to the church at Ephesus, following this slide from fire to fumes, begins with a compliment on their actions. However, as we read further, we discover that these were only actions, not necessarily love.

But actions should have been enough, right? No. Think about your own marriage for a moment. Has your spouse ever acted in line with how a marriage should function, and yet you sensed the actions

What we do doesn't always reveal the heart behind it, but those closest to us—God and our spouses—know our hearts, regardless of what is done.

were more out of duty than out of a heart of love? Or consider whether you've done something similar. What we do doesn't always reveal the heart behind it, but those closest to us—God and our spouses—know our hearts, regardless of what is done.

Let's look at how this unfolds for the church of Ephesus, where what started out as a strong commendation for doing great things ended up revealing an empty heart beneath it all:

> I know your deeds and your toil and perseverance, and that you
> cannot tolerate evil men, and you put to the test those who call
> themselves apostles, and they are not, and you found them to be false;
> and you have perseverance and have endured for My name's sake, and
> have not grown weary. (Revelation 2:2–3)

To set the stage, the church of Ephesus had developed into a serving church. What began with a passionate fire for the Lord had produced what most would consider great things. The Ephesian believers were spiritual bumblebees. Everyone was in a ministry, engaged in activity, and doing something to promote good while keeping out evil. They persevered and didn't abandon their roles. The church members had standards and kept them. They wouldn't throw in the towel in spite of ongoing challenges that would have made the best of us weary. Despite it all, the church of Ephesus hung tough.

Before we read about the heart behind their actions, let's overlay this biblical example on top of the marriage scenario. If we were to put this passage in the context of marriage, these are husbands and wives who check items off their to-do lists. They read the Word, play with the kids, and perform the actions that ought to make for a strong home. They don't give in to laziness or selfishness but rather seek to serve. And as we read in this passage, all of that is good. The church at Ephesus was commended for these things and more, and married couples who do similar things should be commended as well.

However, there is a "but." After all of the accolades and praise for a job well done, God follows His message to the church with a small conjunction that had a large meaning: "*But* I have this against you, that you have left your first love" (Revelation 2:4). In other words, "Yes, church at Ephesus, you have done a lot of great stuff. Yes, you are the recipient of many compliments. *But* I have one major criticism that cancels out the rest: You have left your first love. A lot of things may be going right, but this one wrong thing is majorly wrong."

Let's examine this for a moment, because this apparently means that you can be serving, doing, giving, and more but not have your first love. You can be sacrificing but not have your first love. You can be steadfast and even suffer but not have your first love. Despite all of this, something was missing in the church at Ephesus.

When we read this passage in Revelation, it is easy to overlook a critical distinction. The believers in Ephesus weren't told that they had no love. God didn't say, "Church at Ephesus, you don't love Me." He said, "You have left your *first* love." Notice the word *first*.

First love is different from love. First love always includes something that general agape love may not: passion. Think back to the first time you fell in love. Do you remember the fire inside of you? That blaze dominated your thoughts and actions. When you were in first love, you couldn't get off the phone. The two of you would talk all night long, even when you were about to fall asleep. First love always involves desire.

The church at Ephesus wasn't missing anything in their program; they just had a program without any fire. They had a program without any passion. This is similar to what a lot of wives experience on Valentine's Day. Every year this holiday of love rolls around, placing a long list of expectations on the husbands. Trust me, I know. The problem is that far too many husbands give their wives a card, take them out to dinner, and tell them nice things simply because they know that if they don't do those things, and more, they'll be in the doghouse for the next year.

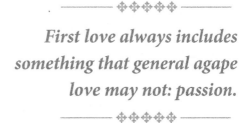

First love always includes something that general agape love may not: passion.

It's an expectation of service that far too often gets fulfilled without the fire. A husband can say, "Well, baby, I did A, B, and C." He can articulate his programmatic clarity thoroughly, and yet something is missing.

Now remember that first love and those times when there might not have even been enough money for a card and dinner, and the gift may have been from a store ending in "mart." Still, it was all more than satisfying because it was attached to the passion of first love.

First love means more than money. First love is rooted in motivation more than movement. When the church at Ephesus left their first love, they degenerated into religion at the expense of relationship. Yet God's first concern with them—and with you and me—was their devotion. Just as your first concern with your spouse is devotion. Because when you have fire, you will also have the actions. You can do the actions without the fire, but when the fire dies in light of the work schedule, performance, or even duty, the actions ring empty.

I remember one time I was at a hotel and picked up an apple sitting in a bowl of fruit. It looked juicy and ripe, but when I bit into it, I discovered that it was a wax apple. Before I bit into it, it looked like the nicest, juiciest apple I had ever seen, tempting me up there on the counter as I checked in. That apple looked real. But it wasn't authentic.

In other words, you can look happily married. You can look as if you have a close family. You can look as though you do all the right things. But you may still be in a miserable situation simply because you have left your first love. Your relationship is no longer your focus, and you have resorted to carrying out the program and system called marriage.

Back before seat belts were required, you could tell the couples who were in their first-love stage, because both of them were behind the wheel, not just the driver. The woman would be all up under her man. You could also tell those couples who had left their first love, because she would be sitting as close to the door as possible.

What Now?

Thankfully God didn't leave the church at Ephesus with the problem. He offered them a solution. The good news for married couples who may have lost their first love is that lost love can be regained. The pilot light can be relit. The flame can be reignited. Sure, it doesn't just happen, but it's possible. God gives us three steps to help make it happen: Remember. Repent. Repeat.

Remember

The pathway to rekindling the passion of your first love is to remember from whence you once came: "Therefore remember from where you have fallen" (Revelation 2:5). Go back in time to that place when you probably didn't have much money, you lived in an apartment, and there was only one car. You barely had enough to make ends meet, but you had more than enough to make life matter—you had first love. Go back to those times when you dated and fantasized about each other. When you relived your kisses in your mind. Take a trip back in time and remember what it felt like to hold hands when sitting on the couch. Remember what those conversations were like when you explored the depths of each other's hearts and minds. Remember how he used to make you laugh without even trying, and

Remember how he used to make you laugh without even trying, and how you turned his head when you would walk into the room.

how you turned his head when you would walk into the room. Remember when submission was done without even asking—gladly, simply because you wanted to please him. And he wrapped you in his arms every night simply because he could.

The instruction God gave to the church at Ephesus—to remember from where they had fallen—is the same instruction I'm giving to you as a married couple who may have lost your passion. You can't tell me that you got married without passion and fire, desire and delight. If it was there then, you can revive it. Begin by remembering what it was like. Rehearse this in your mind, because what we think affects what we do and say.

If you are thinking thoughts that remember the fire, it will have a profound effect on how you treat your spouse now. It's going to come out in what you say and don't say—and the heart in which things are done. Remember your first love—how you felt. Feel those feelings again, even if they are just a memory now. The more you allow yourself to feel them, the more likely they are to return. Don't allow the pain and disappointments that plague every marriage—yours is no exception—to block these emotions of first love. When you feel pain, bitterness, or even simple apathy, quickly focus on remembering the feelings of first love. Do this enough times, and it will become habit. In fact, discuss with your mate how things used to be. That will help bring back your memory.

Repent

The next thing we are told to do in our relationship with God is to repent. Now the last time I checked, there's only one thing you repent of in the Bible, and that is sin. So guess what? Leaving your first love for God is considered a sin. It's not just a circumstance. Similarly, losing your love for your spouse is also a sin, because we are commanded to love in Scripture—not only others in general but our spouses in particular (Mark 12:31; Ephesians 5:25; Colossians 3:19).

Whenever there is a physical or emotional departure from the established sanctity of the marriage union, sin has been introduced. And whenever there is sin, repentance is a necessary part of restoration. Whether that repentance comes quietly between you and God during your prayer time or you share it with your spouse isn't as important as being sure that it happens from an authentic place within you. Not only that, but repentance also involves an action. Repentance means to go in the opposite direction. It means to turn around, to reverse course.

Some of the issues and challenges we face in our relationships as married couples may be unfixable. There may be too much hurt, pain, and anguish involved. All of the patching up in the world can't solve certain things, simply because the wear and tear is too deep. In situations like this, when you can't patch up a window, door, roof, or part of a building, an implosion is necessary. Again, in an implosion, dynamite is placed in a building to collapse it.

> *Some of the issues and challenges we face in our relationships as married couples may be unfixable.*

Do you know why construction crews collapse a building? To put something new in its spot. They tear the building down in order to clear the way for something fresh. Often, couples will spend all of their time and emotional energy trying to fix an argument or a situation that is so messed up it can't be fixed. So what do you have to do in those situations? You have to discover how to create something brand new. Consider the beautiful thing about a calculator. When you put in the wrong number, you don't have to unravel it. You simply push "clear" and start again.

It is that willingness to start again by going back to the things involved in first love that can help married couples regain their lost zeal. Rather than remaining stuck in the muck that piles up over time, consider letting that go and focusing your energy on doing, thinking, and feeling the things you once did, thought, and felt at the start. Seek to rewin, rewoo, redate, and relove your spouse. Approach your spouse like you did when you didn't have him or her tied up for life. Far too often we presume on our spouses because we expect them to be there. In a sense, we take advantage of their presence and forget to cherish the things about them that we did at the start.

Repeat

One of the ways to rekindle your relationship is to ask yourself, "Would I have said that or acted this way when we were dating?" If the answer is no, then why would you do it now? Honor your spouse with the same attentiveness and love you showed at the start, and you will experience a renewal in your relationship.

God has taken us from step 1, which is to remember, to step 2, which is to repent. The last step in returning to our first love is to repeat. God tells us to "do the deeds you did at first" (Revelation 2:5).

Most couples don't date much after they get married. Demands and schedules start to weigh down the relationship, which makes it more and more difficult to date. The modern form of dating is nothing like what happened in Bible times. These days, in America and many other Western countries, people date to get to know someone so they can decide whether they will marry one day. But that's not what we discover in Scripture. In biblical culture, we don't find dating to marry but rather marrying to date. It's the opposite.

A lot of the marriages in biblical times were arranged. The parents often decided whom their children would marry. One reason was that marriage was supposed to be the foundation from which a couple built the relationship, not that which killed it.

> *One of the ways to rekindle your relationship is to ask yourself, "Would I have said that or acted this way when we were dating?"*

As you seek to rekindle the love in your marriage, do the things you used to do when you dated. Repeat those things you did when you were relationship-driven, not program-driven. Repeat special words, kind gestures, dressing up, and remembering the other person's favorite food. Repeat seeking out things to do that you both will enjoy, carving out time when there is none to be had, trying to look your best. Repeat listening when you've heard that story several times before. Or laughing when the joke really isn't that funny. Repeat noticing what it is about your spouse that sets him or her apart from the rest, and then point it out. Repeat these things and more, and you will rekindle your first love.

————— ✥✥✥✥✥ —————

Make every attempt to remember, repent, and repeat to rekindle that which caused you to marry in the first place.

————— ✥✥✥✥✥ —————

Relationships are powerful. The marriage relationship is one of the most intimate, rewarding experiences in life—if you treat it with the honor, attention, and love it deserves. Nourish each other as you first did. Guard yourselves from the "program" of marriage. Make every attempt to remember, repent, and repeat to rekindle that which caused you to marry in the first place.

❖❖❖❖❖❖

TURNING WATER INTO WINE

IT'S FITTING THAT CHRIST would give us one of our greatest lessons on marriage through something He did at a wedding. If you've spent any time in the church at all, or any time studying your Bible, you are probably familiar with the wedding where Jesus turned water into wine. This well-known miracle offers us a number of lessons on faith, trust, and timing. Yet something new jumped out at me recently when I was preaching on this gospel passage. Couched within the conversations and circumstances at this wedding ceremony is hidden a critical principle for kingdom couples.

It's fitting that Christ would give us one of our greatest lessons on marriage through something He did at a wedding.

To set the stage, weddings in Bible days were enormous social events. Unlike today, where we focus on an afternoon or evening ceremony along with a reception and then throw some rice and call it a day, these historical weddings would last a week. People traveled great distances to be a part of them, making the parents of the bride responsible not only for putting on a good ceremony but also for throwing a great party for an extended length of time.

There was food, music, laughter, and of course, wine. Yet at this particular wedding recorded in John 2, the hosts faced something unimaginable. The wine had run dry, literally. It was gone. Talk about a wedding crasher! This reality was about to cast a somber tone over what was supposed to be a festive occasion.

That's when Jesus's mother decided to do something about it. She approached her Son and said, "They have no wine" (verse 3). Translation, "Boy, do something! I know who You are." It kind of makes me think of Clark Kent's mother whispering in his ear at a time of crisis, "Wouldn't now be a good time to find a phone booth?"

Apparently Jesus didn't take to His mom telling Him what to do with regard to His deity, so He replied, "Woman, what does that have to do with us? My hour has not yet come" (verse 4). Translation: "Relax, this isn't our problem."

But just as any good son might do, after Christ shrugged His shoulders to His mom's request, He went ahead and handled it anyway. Nothing in His words would have given His mom the idea that He was going to do something, so perhaps it was His nonverbals—a twinkle in His eye or a sigh in His voice when He told her that His time had not yet come. Whatever it was, she knew her Son was going to handle the situation, because her next words to the servants were "Whatever He says to you, do it" (verse 5).

A successful kingdom marriage can be boiled down to that one phrase: "Whatever He says to you, do it."

That's an important statement. It's also a statement that often goes unnoticed and unheeded in our everyday lives. Sure, we understand that Mary, the mother of Jesus, told the servants to do whatever Jesus asked them to do. But if we were to apply her advice to our lives and marriages, how much better off would we be? A successful kingdom marriage can be boiled down to that one phrase: "Whatever He says to you, do it."

Although that is fundamentally what I want to leave you with as we end our time together, there's more. As we keep reading in John 2, we see that Jesus sent the servants to fill up the six stone pots with water. I don't know about you, but that seems like a ridiculous thing to ask someone who's short of wine to do. I wonder what the servants were thinking as they headed down to the well to fill up the empty pots with water. Surely they knew that their master wanted wine for his guests. But in accordance with what Mary had instructed them to do, they went.

Somewhere between the well and the headwaiter, the water became wine. Not just any wine either, because the headwaiter exclaimed to the bridegroom, "Every man serves the good wine first, and when the people have drunk freely, then he serves the poorer wine; but you have kept the good wine until now" (verse 10). In other words, it was tradi-

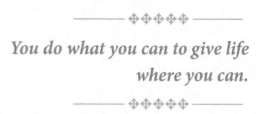

You do what you can to give life where you can.

tion to serve the best wine first while people's minds were still sharp and their taste buds were fresh. After a bit of drinking, the servants would pull out the cheaper wine. But when Jesus performed His miracle, His wine outdid them all.

Likewise, when God does a supernatural work in your marriage in response to your acting in faith and doing whatever He says to do, even the things that look empty right now will be filled with something better than you could ever have expected, and something sweeter than you might ever have imagined.

I've counseled enough couples to know that far too many of the loneliest people on this planet wear a wedding ring on their fingers. Their relationships feel empty, without even a drop of hope for improvement. Husbands and wives are worn out, depleted, spent. Yet in spite of the emptiness or the lack you may feel in your marriage, I want you to do one thing: Fill that emptiness with water. Fill it with what you have access to, even if it doesn't look as if what you do will change anything at all. Don't wait for your spouse to fill it. You go to the well, and input the water of life into your empty relationship. Water is a life-giving source, so whatever you can do to nourish your marriage, do that now.

You might be saying, "But Tony, my husband doesn't meet my needs. He's always gone. He doesn't talk to me anymore." I hear you, and I understand. But you fill that emptiness with water. You do what you can to give life where you can.

Or you could be saying, "Tony, she's always with the kids or busy with her activities. I've lost the woman I fell in love with. She doesn't respect me anymore or meet my needs." That could also be true. But fill that emptiness with water.

The water did not get turned into wine until the empty pots were filled. That was the condition upon which this miracle depended. The servants had to go to the well and do the ridiculous thing. They had to do that which no one in his right mind would have ever thought would produce wine. But they did it anyway, because that's what Jesus said to do.

Sometimes God asks us to do the ridiculous in our marriages in order to reveal our faith in Him. You may be harboring bitterness and resentment toward your spouse right now, but fill that relationship with love—intentional acts of patience, kindness, and goodness. Bite your tongue and offer love. God will transform your faith into wine. In the Bible, wine is a symbol of joy. What Jesus did at the wedding was turn emptiness into joy.

If couples would spend as much time in prayer for their spouses as they do complaining, debating, berating, and demanding, they would experience the vibrant, abundant marriages God intended for them to have.

Christ told His mother that His time had not yet come. He didn't perform this miracle for the public—no one even knew, other than the servants and His mom. Even the headwaiter had no idea where the wine came from, as we saw in his response to the bridegroom when he tasted the wine. But Christ did the miracle nonetheless, and He'll do the same for you. When you spend private time with the Lord seeking what He wants you to do behind the scenes, He can bring joy where there is lack. Take to the Lord all the public complaints about your spouse, all the public discussions with your friends, and even the public actions that reveal to others the emptiness of your marriage and ask Him to heal your relationship.

If couples would spend as much time in prayer for their spouses as they do complaining, debating, berating, and demanding, they would experience the vibrant, abundant marriages God intended for them to have. But how can you hear what Christ would have you do above the noise of your own conflict or pain?

My hope as we close this study on kingdom couples is that you will take the principles taught in Scripture and apply them to yourself and your marriage. Wherever your spouse lacks these principles, take that to the Lord in prayer and ask Him to show you what He wants you to do, not what He wants your spouse to do. Filling pots with water was a ridiculous request too, so don't second-guess what God tells you to do. Just do it.

It might be a kind word or a closed mouth when you feel like lashing out. It could be greater patience or more respect for what is right and good in your relationship. It may be that you need to remember, repent, and repeat what you did when you first dated and return to that first love. Or perhaps you need to humbly relinquish the control you feel you have a right to over how your spouse treats or responds to you. It could be any number of things, or even all of the above. But one thing is for sure, a rewarding kingdom marriage begins with you.

Yes, it takes two, but just as no one could have predicted that water would be turned into wine, the way God desires and designs to mature and grow your spouse for a deeper relationship with you is His call. His ways are beyond our understanding (Isaiah 55:8–9). Leave that up to Him, and like the servants at the wedding, do whatever He tells you to do. Then sit back and take a sip. You may think it is the end, but this party is just getting started.

He has saved your best for last!

THE URBAN ALTERNATIVE

Dr. Tony Evans' ministry The Urban Alternative (TUA) *equips, empowers,* and *unites* Christians to impact *individuals, families, churches,* and *communities* through a thoroughly Kingdom agenda worldview. In teaching truth, we seek to transform lives.

The core cause of the problems we face in our personal lives, homes, churches, and societies is a spiritual one; therefore, the only way to address it is spiritually. We've tried a political, social, economic, and even a religious agenda.

It's time for a *Kingdom agenda.*

> *The Kingdom agenda can be defined as the visible manifestation*
> *of the comprehensive rule of God over every area of life.*

The unifying central theme throughout the Bible is the glory of God and the advancement of His kingdom. The conjoining thread from Genesis to Revelation—from beginning to end—is focused on one thing: God's glory through advancing God's kingdom.

When you do not have that theme, the Bible becomes disconnected stories that are great for inspiration but seem to be unrelated in purpose and direction. The Bible exists to share God's movement in history toward the establishment and expansion of His kingdom highlighting the connectivity throughout which is the kingdom. Understanding that increases the relevancy of this several-thousand-year-old manuscript to your day-to-day living, because the Kingdom is not only then, it is now.

The absence of the kingdom's influence in our personal and family lives, churches, and communities has led to a deterioration in our world of immense proportions:

- People live segmented, compartmentalized lives because they lack God's Kingdom worldview.
- Families disintegrate because they exist for their own satisfaction rather than for the Kingdom.
- Churches are limited in the scope of their impact because they fail to comprehend that the goal of the church is not the church itself, but the Kingdom.
- Communities have nowhere to turn to find real solutions for real people who have real problems, because the church has become divided, ingrown, and unable to transform the cultural landscape in any relevant way.

The Kingdom agenda offers us a way to see and live life with a solid hope by optimizing the solutions of heaven. When God, and His rule, is no longer the final and authoritative standard under which all else falls, order and hope leaves with Him. But the reverse of that is true as well: As long as you have God, you have hope. If God is still in the picture, and as long as His agenda is still on the table, it's not over.

Even if relationships collapse, God will sustain you. Even if finances dwindle, God will keep you. Even if dreams die, God will revive you. As long as God, and His rule, is still the overarching rule in your life, family, church, and community, there is always hope.

Our world needs the King's agenda. Our churches need the King's agenda. Our families need the King's agenda.

In many major cities, there is a loop that drivers can take when they want to get somewhere on the other side of the city, but don't necessarily want to head straight through downtown. This loop will take you close enough to the city so that you can see its towering buildings and skyline, but not close enough to actually experience it.

This is precisely what we, as a culture, have done with God. We have put Him on the "loop" of our personal, family, church, and community lives. He's close enough to be at hand should we need Him in an emergency, but far enough away that He can't be the center of who we are.

We want God on the "loop," not the King of the Bible who comes downtown into the very heart of our ways. Leaving God on the "loop" brings about dire consequences, as we have seen in our own lives and with others. But when we make God, and His rule, the centerpiece of all we think, do, or say, it is then that we will experience Him in the way He longs to be experienced by us.

He wants us to be kingdom people with kingdom minds set on fulfilling His kingdom's purposes. He wants us to pray, as Jesus did, "Not my will, but Thy will be done." Because His is the kingdom, the power, and the glory.

There is only one God, and we are not Him. As King and Creator, God calls the shots. It is only when we align ourselves underneath His comprehensive hand that we will access His full power and authority in all spheres of life: personal, familial, church, and community.

As we learn how to govern ourselves under God, we then transform the institutions of family, church, and society from a biblically based kingdom worldview.

Under Him, we touch heaven and change earth.

To achieve our goal we use a variety of strategies, approaches, and resources for reaching and equipping as many people as possible.

BROADCAST MEDIA

Millions of individuals experience *The Alternative with Dr. Tony Evans* through the daily radio broadcast playing on nearly one thousand radio outlets and in over one hundred countries. The broadcast can also be seen on several television networks and is viewable online at TonyEvans.org. You can also listen to or view the daily broadcast by downloading the Tony Evans app for free in the App store. Over four million message downloads occur each year.

LEADERSHIP TRAINING

The *Tony Evans Training Center* (TETC) facilitates educational programming that embodies the ministry philosophy of Dr. Tony Evans as expressed through the Kingdom agenda. The training courses focus on leadership development and discipleship in the following five tracks:

- Bible and Theology
- Personal Growth
- Family and Relationships
- Church Health and Leadership Development
- Society and Community Impact Strategies

The TETC program includes courses for both local and online students. Furthermore, TETC programming includes course work for non-student attendees. Pastors, Christian leaders, and Christian laity, both local and at a distance, can seek out The Kingdom Agenda Certificate for personal, spiritual, and professional development. Some courses are valued for CEU (Continuing Education Unit) credit as well as viable in transferring for college credit with our partner school(s).

Kingdom Agenda Pastors (KAP) provides a viable network for like-minded pastors who embrace the Kingdom agenda philosophy. Pastors have the opportunity to go deeper with Dr. Tony Evans as they are given greater biblical knowledge, practical applications, and resources to impact individuals, families, churches, and communities. KAP welcomes senior and associate pastors of all churches. KAP also offers an annual Summit held each year in Dallas with intensive seminars, workshops, and resources.

Pastors' Wives Ministry, founded by Dr. Lois Evans, provides counsel, encouragement, and spiritual resources for pastors' wives as they serve with their husbands in the ministry. A primary focus of the ministry is the KAP Summit that offers senior pastors' wives a safe place to reflect, renew, and relax along with training in personal development, spiritual growth, and care for their emotional and physical well-being.

COMMUNITY IMPACT

National Church Adopt-A-School Initiative (NCAASI) prepares churches across the country to impact communities by using public schools as the primary vehicle for effecting positive social change in urban youth and families. Leaders of churches, school districts, faith-based organizations, and other nonprofit organizations are equipped with the knowledge and tools to forge partnerships and build strong social service delivery systems. This training is based on the comprehensive church-based community impact strategy conducted by Oak Cliff Bible Fellowship. It addresses such areas as economic development, education, housing, health revitalization, family renewal, and racial reconciliation. We assist churches in tailoring the model to meet specific needs of their communities while simultaneously addressing the spiritual and moral frame of reference. Training events are held annually in the Dallas area at Oak Cliff Bible Fellowship.

Athlete's Impact (AI) exists as an outreach both into and through the sports arena. Coaches are often the most influential factor in young people's lives, even ahead of their parents. With the growing rise of fatherlessness in our culture, more young people are looking to their coaches for guidance, character development, practical needs, and hope. Athletes are next on the influencer scale after coaches. Athletes (whether professional or amateur) influence younger athletes and kids within their spheres of impact. Knowing this, we have made it our aim to equip and train coaches and athletes on how to live out and utilize their God-given roles for the benefit of the Kingdom. We aim to do this through our iCoach App and weCoach Football Conference as well as resources such as *The Playbook: A Life Strategy Guide for Athletes.*

RESOURCE DEVELOPMENT

We are fostering lifelong learning partnerships with the people we serve by providing a variety of published materials. Dr. Evans has published more than one hundred unique titles based on over forty years of preaching, whether that is in booklet, book, or Bible study format. The goal is to strengthen individuals in their walk with God and service to others.

For more information
and a complimentary copy of Dr. Evans' devotional newsletter,
call (800) 800-3222;
or write TUA at PO Box 4000, Dallas, TX 75208;
or visit us online at www.TonyEvans.org.

ACKNOWLEDGMENTS

✦✦✦✦✦✦

I WANT TO EXPRESS my heartfelt gratitude to Focus on the Family and Tyndale House Publishers for the support, commitment, and excellence they have given to this work.

SCRIPTURE INDEX

NEW TESTAMENT

NOTES

CHAPTER 1: ORIGIN

1. Sarah Pruitt, "5 Things You May Not Know About Queen Victoria," History in the Headlines, History.com, June 28, 2013, http://www.history.com /news/5-things-you-may-not-know-about-queen-victoria.

2. Robert McNamara, "Prince Albert, Husband of Queen Victoria," About.com, accessed December 5, 2015, http://history1800s.about.com/od/leaders/a/prince-albert-html.htm.

3. "How Many Children Did Queen Victoria Have and Who Was the Oldest?," Biographies, YourDictionary.com, accessed December 5, 2015, http://biography.yourdictionary.com /articles/children-queen-victoria-who-oldest.html.

4. Pruitt, "5 Things You May Not Know About Queen Victoria."

CHAPTER 2: ORDER

1. Statistics from US Department of State, cited in David A. Sleet, David J. Ederer, and Michael F. Ballesteros, "The Pre-Travel Consultation: Injury Prevention," in *CDC Health Information for International Travel* (Washington, DC: Centers for Disease Control and Prevention, 2016), chapter 2, http://wwwnc.cdc.gov/travel/yellowbook/2016/the-pre-travel-consultation /injury-prevention.

2. Statistic cited in "Vehicle Accidents Put U.S. Citizens Traveling in Foreign Countries at Risk," EuropAssistance-USA.com, October 17, 2013, http://www.europassistance-usa.com /blog/archives/vehicle-accidents-put-u-s-citizens-traveling-in-foreign-countries-at-risk/.

CHAPTER 5: ONENESS

1. *Runaway Bride*, directed by Garry Marshall (Paramount Pictures, 1999).

2. Summary from Ken Sande, *The Peacemaker: A Biblical Guide to Resolving Personal Conflict*, 3d ed. (Grand Rapids: Baker Books, 2004), 12–13.

CHAPTER 6: ROLES

1. "50 Women You Should Know," *Christianity Today* 56, no. 9 (October 19, 2012), http:// www.christianitytoday.com/ct/2012/october/50-women-you-should-know.html.

2. *Strong's Concordance*, s.v. Hebrew 5828 *ezer*, http://biblehub.com/hebrew/5828.htm.

3. *Strong's Concordance*, s.v. Hebrew 5048 *kenegdo*, root *neged*, http://biblehub.com /hebrew/5048.htm.

4. Ibid.

CHAPTER 7: RESOLUTIONS

1. Gary Thomas, *Sacred Marriage* (Grand Rapids: Zondervan, 2000), 13.

2. Erin Prater, "Chronic Illness in Marriage," Chronic Illness in Marriage Series, Pt. 1, 2008, FocusontheFamily.com, http://www.focusonthefamily.com /marriage/facing-crisis/chronic-illness/chronic-illness-in-marriage.

CHAPTER 8: REQUESTS

1. *War Room*, directed by Alex Kendrick (Provident Films, 2015).

2. Stu Woo, "The Great Super Bowl Bed Check," *Wall Street Journal*, Life and Culture, January 31, 2015, http://www.wsj.com/articles/the-great-super-bowl-bed-check-1422729297.

CHAPTER 10: RESOURCES

1. Abraham Lincoln, "Proclamation Appointing a National Fast Day," speech, Washington, DC, March 30, 1863, http://www.abrahamlincolnonline.org/lincoln/speeches/fast.htm.

CHAPTER 11: ROMANCE

1. Sheril Kirshenbaum, "Sealed with a Kiss—and Neuroscience," *Washington Post*, December 26, 2010, http://www.washingtonpost.com/wp-dyn/content/article/2010/12/23 /AR2010122304771.html, emphasis added.

2. Ibid.

3. Helen Fisher, "The Brain in Love," speech, TED Talks, February 2008, https://www.ted.com /talks/helen_fisher_studies_the_brain_in_love/transcript?language=en.

4. Kirshenbaum, "Sealed with a Kiss."

5. Ibid.

6. *Strong's Concordance*, s.v. Hebrew 3045 *yada*, http://biblehub.com/hebrew/3045.htm.

7. *Strong's Concordance*, s.v. Greek 4203 *porneuō*, http://biblehub.com/greek/4203.htm.

8. *Strong's Concordance*, s.v. Hebrew 7901 *shakab*, http://biblehub.com/hebrew/7901.htm.

9. Adam Hadhazy, "Do Pheromones Play a Role in Our Sex Lives?" *Scientific American*, February 13, 2012, http://www.scientificamerican.com/article/pheromones-sex-lives/.

10. Susan Rako and Joan Friebely, "Pheromonal Influences on Sociosexual Behavior in Postmenopausal Women," *Journal of Sex Research* 41, no. 4 (November 2004): 372–380, http://www.jstor.org/stable/pdf/3813545. pdf?acceptTC=true&seq=1#page_scan_tab_contents.

11. Study published in Amanda Denes, "The Science of Pillow Talk," *UConn Today*, December 27, 2013, http://today.uconn.edu/2013/12/the-science-of-pillow-talk/.

12. Fisher, "The Brain in Love."

13. *Strong's Concordance*, s.v. Greek 2853 *kollaō*, http://biblehub.com/greek/2853.htm.

Kingdom Marriage Book and *Kingdom Marriage Group Video Experience* $10 Rebate

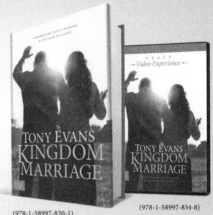

GET A $10 REBATE

when you purchase both the *Kingdom Marriage Group Video Experience* and *Kingdom Marriage* hardcover book. Both titles must be purchased at a retail store to qualify. Simply return the completed rebate form (original or photocopy), the original dated store receipt(s) for both products, and the UPC bar code from both packages (original or photocopy) to: Kingdom Marriage Rebate, Attn. Customer Service, 351 Executive Dr., Carol Stream, IL 60188.

(978-1-58997-820-1)

(978-1-58997-834-8)

NAME _____

ADDRESS _____

CITY _____ STATE _____ ZIP _____

E-MAIL ADDRESS _____

STORE WHERE PURCHASED _____

SIGNATURE _____

THE KINGDOM SERIES
FROM DR. TONY EVANS

MORE RESOURCES TO GROW YOUR FAITH AND FURTHER GOD'S KINGDOM!

KINGDOM MAN
978-1-58997-685-6

KINGDOM MAN
DEVOTIONAL
978-1-62405-121-0

KINGDOM WOMAN
978-1-58997-743-3

KINGDOM WOMAN
DEVOTIONAL
978-1-62405-122-7

KINGDOM WOMAN
VIDEO STUDY
978-1-62405-209-5

RAISING KINGDOM KIDS
978-1-58997-784-6

RAISING KINGDOM KIDS
DEVOTIONAL
978-1-62405-409-9

RAISING KINGDOM KIDS
VIDEO STUDY
978-1-62405-407-5

More Resources to Help You Thrive in Marriage and Life

Starting now, this could be your best day, week, month, or year! Discover ways to express your needs, embrace your purpose, and love more fully. We offer life-transforming books, e-books, videos, devotionals, study guides, audiobooks, and audio dramas to equip you for God's calling on your life. Visit your favorite retailer, or go to **FocusOnTheFamily.com/resources**.

Meet the rest of the family

Expert advice on parenting and marriage ...
spiritual growth ... powerful personal stories ...

Focus on the Family's collection of inspiring, practical resources can help your family grow closer to God—and each other—than ever before. Whichever format you need—video, audio, book, or e-book—we have something for you. Discover how to help your family thrive with books, DVDs, and more at **FocusOnTheFamily.com/resources**.

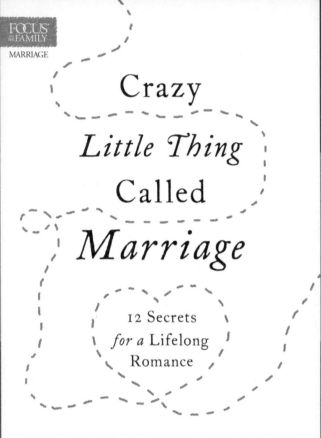